Microsoft Dynamics CRM 2011 Scripting Cookbook

Over 50 recipes to extend system customization in
Dynamics CRM 2011 through client-side scripting

Nicolae Tarla

[PACKT] enterprise
PUBLISHING   professional expertise distilled

BIRMINGHAM - MUMBAI

Microsoft Dynamics CRM 2011 Scripting Cookbook

First published: March 2013

Production Reference: 1150313

Published by Packt Publishing Ltd.
Livery Place
35 Livery Street
Birmingham B3 2PB, UK.

ISBN 978-1-84968-882-6

www.packtpub.com

Cover Image by Artie Ng (artherng@yahoo.com.au)

Credits

Author

Nicolae Tarla

Reviewers

Michael G. Ferreira

Sandor Schellenberg

Tanguy TOUZARD

Acquisition Editor

Mary Nadar

Lead Technical Editor

Susmita Panda

Technical Editors

Sharvari Baet

Devdutt Kulkarni

Dennis John

Project Coordinator

Esha Thakker

Proofreaders

Sandra Hopper

Samantha Lyon

Lydia May Morris

Indexer

Tejal R. Soni

Graphics

Aparna Bhagat

Production Coordinators

Aparna Bhagat

Prachali Bhiwandkar

Cover Work

Aparna Bhagat

About the Author

Nicolae Tarla is a Senior Consultant in a Solutions Architect role. He has worked on various mid-size to enterprise-level Dynamics CRM and SharePoint solutions for both the private and public sectors. He has been delivering Microsoft Dynamics CRM solutions since the version 3.0 of the product. Nicolae also participated as a technical reviewer on the book *Microsoft Dynamics CRM 2011: Dashboards Cookbook*.

I would like to thank my wife and daughter, who put up with the hectic schedule and the long nights and weekends consumed over the last few months on this project. They both fully supported me from start to finish. I want to give an additional thank you to Mark for introducing me to the writing process and asking me the dreaded question: When are you writing yours? That was the starting point.

About the Reviewers

Michael G. Ferreira, is a diverse "hands on" leader, entrepreneur, and executive consultant with 20 years of widely diverse business and technology leadership experience. He has crafted client/vendor/partner relationships, advisory services, managed large project portfolios, directed product development, implemented transformation change, and pioneered new service delivery techniques.

Since 2003 (Microsoft Dynamics CRM 1.0 beta), Michael has been working with a diverse range of customers and partner organizations (start-up to enterprise; across industries). He has proposed, lead, architected, and deployed over 100+ Microsoft CRM-based technology solutions ranging from out-of-the-box configurations to product upgrades to very complex integrated multi-channel service delivery platforms (CRM, ERP, Portal, Mobile, Social, BI/DW with integration).

Beyond implementation, Michael has played a key role in building the Microsoft CRM partner and consultant community, having helped launch seven organizational practices/delivery teams as well as building and selling his own uniquely positioned Microsoft-based technology solutions provider offering professional and managed services, vertical software/platform-as-a-service products, and hardware and software sales.

I'd like to thank Packt Publishing for letting me participate and my wife for her support throughout the process.

Sandor Schellenberg is the owner and founder of friendlyITsolutions (`http://www.friendlyitsolutions.nl/`), which mainly focuses on Microsoft Dynamics CRM and related software in the Microsoft stack. He is a Senior Microsoft Dynamics CRM Consultant/ Solution Architect and specializes in data migrations and integrations.

In autumn of 2009 his work was recognized and rewarded with an invitation to the Scribe Software MVP Program. In 2013 he was rewarded for a fifth time for the program.

His roots in Microsoft-based Internet technologies go back more than 15 years, and since 2005 he has specialized in Microsoft Dynamics CRM. Starting with his first guest post on the blog of Menno te Koppele, he then decided to start his own blog, Friendly Microsoft CRM Monster (`http://www.friendlycrmonster.com/`), a blog with a wink. The blog is widely read in the Dynamics CRM community and focused mainly on Microsoft Dynamics CRM technical and integration/migration topics. He is also the author of several "musings" at `msdynamics.com`, where he writes about common topics that have to be faced during implementations of Dynamics CRM.

He has experience with implementing Dynamics CRM in several branches and companies in the small to midsize segment, but also in the enterprise segment. Migrations and integrations are not only within the Microsoft stack, but also with widely used software of other vendors including SalesForce, Oracle, and SAP.

Tanguy TOUZARD is a technical consultant and expert on the Microsoft Dynamics CRM application. Since the first version of the application, Tanguy works on integration projects as a developer, consultant, and trainer.

He has expertise in all areas of development and integration around Microsoft Dynamics CRM (JavaScript, Plugins and workflow activities, Reports) and shares his knowledge through Microsoft forums and his blog. He also developed many tools available to the community Dynamics CRM, which made him a Microsoft MVP in the category Dynamics CRM.

www.PacktPub.com

Support files, eBooks, discount offers, and more

You might want to visit www.PacktPub.com for support files and downloads related to your book.

Did you know that Packt offers eBook versions of every book published, with PDF and ePub files available? You can upgrade to the eBook version at www.PacktPub.com and as a print book customer, you are entitled to a discount on the eBook copy. Get in touch with us at service@packtpub.com for more details.

At www.PacktPub.com, you can also read a collection of free technical articles, sign up for a range of free newsletters and receive exclusive discounts and offers on Packt books and eBooks.

http://PacktLib.PacktPub.com

Do you need instant solutions to your IT questions? PacktLib is Packt's online digital book library. Here, you can access, read, and search across Packt's entire library of books.

Why Subscribe?

- ▶ Fully searchable across every book published by Packt
- ▶ Copy and paste, print, and bookmark content
- ▶ On demand and accessible via web browser

Free Access for Packt account holders

If you have an account with Packt at www.PacktPub.com, you can use this to access PacktLib today and view nine entirely free books. Simply use your login credentials for immediate access.

Instant Updates on New Packt Books

Get notified! Find out when new books are published by following @PacktEnterprise on Twitter, or the *Packt Enterprise* Facebook page.

Table of Contents

Preface

This cookbook presents practical and quick solutions that will teach the reader how to customize Dynamics CRM 2011 with minimal effort. The client-side customizations presented in this book work in conjunction with the system customizations to cover a large scale of customizations available for your environment.

The book moves on to more advanced topics as you progress through the various recipes. While the beginning focuses on the basics of working with client side scripting, the later chapters present various solutions you can implement in your environment to help the user see the collected data in new ways.

Taking advantage of various additional client-side libraries, the customizations presented show new ways to extend your Dynamics CRM environment and achieve new levels of customization otherwise not available.

While some of these customizations do have a counterpart in using plugins, the approach presented here is targeted at system customizers and developers that look to achieve the expected results with the minimal effort and in the shortest period of time. In addition, these customizations will add minimal load to the server side, if any.

What this book covers

Each of the chapters in this book adds incremental information, and is based on the prior knowledge gained from previous chapters. For a user that has already knowledge of customizing Dynamics CRM through scripting, you can skip to the recipes of interest, or follow along and see if there is anything new.

Chapter 1, Overview of Dynamics CRM 2011 Customization, introduces the concept of solution packages, and presents the scripting model used for Dynamics CRM 2011. In addition, basic system configuration and settings that work in conjunction with your customizations are presented.

Chapter 2, Scripting Form Fields, covers the most common scripting customizations used when working with various basic form elements. We look at the various field types and how to work with these values.

Chapter 3, Field Validation, includes various validation approaches to enhance the out-of-the-box validation rules. In addition, this chapter presents various approaches to presenting and collecting user input to minimize errors.

Chapter 4, Rules and Events, introduces the reader to the various events presented by Dynamics CRM 2011, as well as working with other form elements available for customization.

Chapter 5, Error Handling, introduces the concept of handling user errors, processing errors, and explains how to prevent the default system behaviors. The advanced topic shows ways to override the default system behavior with custom processing and capturing of user input.

Chapter 6, Debugging, delves into details of working with the scripts and using the available tools to handle various situations where your script misbehaves.

Chapter 7, Extended UI Manipulation, demonstrates ways to introduce visual elements to your forms to highlight form elements and also demonstrates how to handle presenting only the relevant information to a system user.

Chapter 8, Working with Ribbon Elements, is focused on working exclusively with the Ribbon. From adding and removing Ribbon elements, working with events attached to Ribbon elements, and presenting additional information on the Ribbon, most aspect of client-side Ribbon customizations are presented in an easy-to-follow way.

Chapter 9, Extending CRM Using Community JavaScript Libraries, tackles the use of external prebuilt libraries in conjunction with Dynamics CRM 2011. Some of the most popular JavaScript libraries are presented in the context on Dynamics CRM. They will either help you in writing shorter, more efficient scripts, or handle specific form actions.

Chapter 10, Light Social Media Integration, presents a few approaches to bringing information from various social media resources into your Dynamics CRM 2011 environment, with no additional load to server resources. The ways presented here are exclusively client side, and require the system user to have access to these social networks directly.

What you need for this book

In order to complete these short recipes, you will need access to a Dynamics CRM 2011 environment, either Online or On Premise. In addition, you will need a Windows PC with the latest version of Internet Explorer.

For most of these recipes, a text editor such as Notepad is good enough. Of course, using an editor such as Visual Studio will greatly enhance your experience.

Who this book is for

This book targets the new Dynamics CRM 2011 system customizers, the system administrators, as well as the developers. Whether you are new to Dynamics CRM 2011, or a seasoned system customizer or developer, some of these recipes could provide you with additional ways of solving a specific requirement, or give you an alternate approach to more extensive customizations. For developers, these recipes are aimed at showing ways in which some of the plugins can potentially be replaced by light client-side scripts.

This book can also be of value to end users, power users, and business analysts designing a new system. It will provide details on what is necessary with regards to system customization in order to achieve a specific result.

You should be comfortable with generic functionality of Dynamics CRM 2011, or a previous version. While the first chapters introduce you to some of the basic concepts around customization, you should be aware of what the application does out of the box to understand why certain customizations are necessary.

In addition, this book also caters to web designers familiar with standard JavaScript and additional libraries such as jQuery. It presents how these skills can easily be transferred to customizing Dynamics CRM 2011.

Conventions

In this book, you will find a number of styles of text that distinguish between different kinds of information. Here are some examples of these styles, and an explanation of their meaning.

Code words in text, database table names, folder names, filenames, file extensions, pathnames, dummy URLs, user input, and Twitter handles are shown as follows: "Generate a new JScript resource in your solution, named `new_JSUserInput`."

A block of code is set as follows:

```
function checkEmail(emailField)
{
    var email=/^([a-zA-Z0-9_.-])+@([a-zA-Z0-9_.-])+\.([a-zA-Z])+([a-zA-Z])+/;
    if(email.test(emailField))
    {
        // alert("true");
        return true;
    }
}
```

New terms and **important words** are shown in bold. Words that you see on the screen, in menus or dialog boxes for example, appear in the text like this: " Add the **Contact** entity to your solution if not already added."

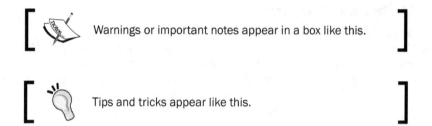

Warnings or important notes appear in a box like this.

Tips and tricks appear like this.

Reader feedback

Feedback from our readers is always welcome. Let us know what you think about this book—what you liked or may have disliked. Reader feedback is important for us to develop titles that you really get the most out of.

To send us general feedback, simply send an e-mail to feedback@packtpub.com, and mention the book title via the subject of your message.

If there is a topic that you have expertise in and you are interested in either writing or contributing to a book, see our author guide on www.packtpub.com/authors.

Customer support

Now that you are the proud owner of a Packt book, we have a number of things to help you to get the most from your purchase.

Downloading the example code

You can download the example code files for all Packt books you have purchased from your account at http://www.packtpub.com. If you purchased this book elsewhere, you can visit http://www.packtpub.com/support and register to have the files e-mailed directly to you.

Errata

Although we have taken every care to ensure the accuracy of our content, mistakes do happen. If you find a mistake in one of our books—maybe a mistake in the text or the code—we would be grateful if you would report this to us. By doing so, you can save other readers from frustration and help us improve subsequent versions of this book. If you find any errata, please report them by visiting http://www.packtpub.com/submit-errata, selecting your book, clicking on the **errata submission form** link, and entering the details of your errata. Once your errata are verified, your submission will be accepted and the errata will be uploaded on our website, or added to any list of existing errata, under the Errata section of that title. Any existing errata can be viewed by selecting your title from http://www.packtpub.com/support.

Piracy

Piracy of copyright material on the Internet is an ongoing problem across all media. At Packt, we take the protection of our copyright and licenses very seriously. If you come across any illegal copies of our works, in any form, on the Internet, please provide us with the location address or website name immediately so that we can pursue a remedy.

Please contact us at `copyright@packtpub.com` with a link to the suspected pirated material.

We appreciate your help in protecting our authors, and our ability to bring you valuable content.

Questions

You can contact us at `questions@packtpub.com` if you are having a problem with any aspect of the book, and we will do our best to address it.

1

Overview of Dynamics CRM 2011 Customization

In this chapter, we will cover:

- ▶ Opening a free 30-day trial of Dynamics CRM 2011 Online
- ▶ Using solutions to package our work
- ▶ Creating and managing entities
- ▶ Creating and managing fields
- ▶ Creating and managing forms
- ▶ Creating and managing scripts
- ▶ Creating and managing other resources
- ▶ Creating and managing workflows
- ▶ Creating and managing dialogs
- ▶ Starting a workflow from a dialog
- ▶ Working with security roles and permissions

Introduction

One of the most useful features of Dynamics CRM is the use of scripting. Version 2011 brings a new object model that is much clearer and concise. Using this object model guarantees that future cumulative updates will not break your scripts, thus it is highly recommended that you convert your old scripts that are using Dynamics CRM 4.0 or standard JavaScript to the new object model as much as possible.

The new object model revolves around the `Xrm.Page` object hierarchy, and brings capabilities to manipulate user interface elements, user forms, and navigational elements. While at first glance the new syntax might seem overwhelming, with some practice it can prove easy to learn.

The object hierarchy of `Xrm.Page` is described in detail on TechNet, at `http://technet. microsoft.com/en-us/library/gg328474`.

Opening a free 30-day trial of Dynamics CRM 2011 Online

In order to follow along with the recipes described in this book, you should sign up for a 30-day trial of Dynamics CRM 2011 Online rather than using an existing production server. This way, all customizations implemented in this environment will not affect your production environment, but they can all be packaged and moved to any other environment once you feel comfortable to do so.

Getting ready

Dynamics CRM Online has now been packaged with Office 365. In order to sign up for a new online instance, you will need to provide a few details as described in the following section.

How to do it...

Creating a new instance of Microsoft Dynamics 2011 Online is a quick and painless task. All you need to figure out is what URL you want to use, and fill in the wizard-driven configuration.

1. Navigate to `http://crm.dynamics.com`.
2. On the **GET STARTED** tile, click on the **Free trial** icon.
3. On the following page click on the **Start your CRM trial** button.
4. The next screen presents you with a form where you provide your personal information as well as the new domain you want to use. This sign-up creates your Office 365 trial account of which Dynamics CRM 2011 is a part.
5. When choosing your domain name, check its availability by clicking on the **Check availability** button. If the selected name is already taken, you will be prompted to select a different one.
6. Pay close attention to the **Country or region** field. This selection cannot be modified once the instance is created, as it sets global parameters for your environment. Note that this will not stop you from configuring additional currencies and territories.

7. Once you confirm the domain name availability, you are prompted to create a user ID. As part of the validation process, your mobile number is required and a text message with a confirmation code is sent.

8. Once all the fields are completed, click on the **create your account** button. You are being directed to the **Administrative** page for your organization. You will observe here the message about the remaining trial period, as well as the navigation to set up and manage your subscription services.

9. The Microsoft Dynamics configuration usually takes a little while longer, and you will see a status of "complete" when done.

10. From here on you are ready to add new users and to navigate to your newly created Dynamics CRM 2011 Online instance by clicking on the **CRM** link.

How it works...

Dynamics CRM 2011 Online is a cloud-based solution offered on the SaaS model. A new instance is provisioned every time a new user goes through this process. With the new model, CRM Online is now part of the Office 365 offering, thus the common familiar account creation process.

There's more...

As mentioned before, certain instance information cannot be modified after they are provisioned during the wizard. These include the organization's name, country, currency, and language. While the default values cannot be modified, additional languages and currencies can be customized, and additional territories can be configured.

Using solutions to package our work

A new concept introduced with Dynamics CRM 2011 is that of solution packages. This allows for code separation, ease of deployment, and cleans up the mess sometimes created in previous version by the large number of possibly unorganized customizations.

Getting ready

In order to follow through with this recipe, log in to your instance of Dynamics CRM 2011 with an account that has either an **administrator** or **system customizer** role. These roles have the necessary out-of-the-box permission to allow you to work with solutions.

How to do it...

A **solution package** is a collection of customizations and configurations that can be generated in an environment and relocated to an additional environment. Creating a new solution is a process that a system administrator or a system customizer can achieve with the following steps:

1. Navigate to **Settings**.

2. Under **Customization**, click on **Solutions**.

3. In the **All Solutions** view, select **New** to create a new solution package.

4. Fill in the mandatory fields, create a new **Publisher** or use the default value, and click on the **Save** icon.

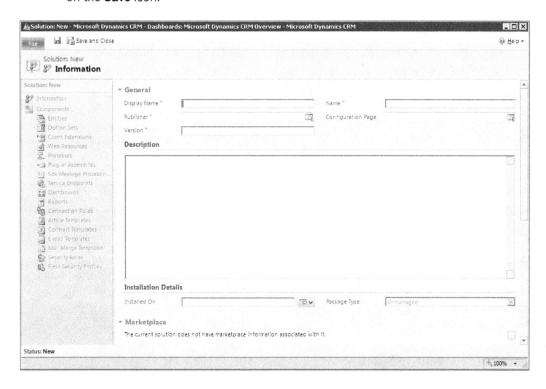

 When developing a solution for the **Marketplace** (as an ISV) you will need to fill in most of the provider information.

Removing a solution is also a very simple process. Select the solution to be removed, and click on the **Delete** icon.

 If this is a managed solution, all solution configurations are cleanly removed from the environment. For an unmanaged solution, the process is not as straight-forward, as the removal of an unmanaged solution will leave behind customizations and trailing components. For additional details on solution see the *Solution model* section of this recipe.

How it works...

Creating a new solution requires you to assign a publisher. By default, each instance of Dynamics CRM 2011 includes a default publisher for the instance. For environments where a solution is to be published to production, create a publisher that includes the organization details of the customizer.

There's more...

Solutions offer additional features such as versioning, which can be essential in tracking progress and deploying to the production environment.

Solution model

Also, with solutions, we have two very important models, a managed and unmanaged solution model. A **managed** solution is a restrictive package, which can only be edited by specific users, and can be cleanly rolled back. An **unmanaged** solution on the other hand is a type of package used mostly for development environments, and it allows various developers to move customizations from one environment to another, while keeping all customizations editable by all users with the proper permissions. Unmanaged solutions, when removed, will not be removed cleanly, and will leave behind traces of customizations. For this reason, they are not the recommended way of deploying to the production environment.

See also

  ▶   For additional details on working with solutions, consult the TechNet library at
      `http://technet.microsoft.com/en-us/library/gg334530.aspx`.

Creating and managing entities

In this recipe, we'll go through the process of creating a new entity, look at how to configure such an entity, and in the end, how to clean up an entity that's not required in our solution package.

All customizations in this book are created as part of a solution. As such, we will be reusing the previously created solution.

Getting ready

In order to proceed, log in to your existing Dynamics CRM 2011 instance and navigate to the solution we created previously.

How to do it...

In the created solution package, we will be adding a new entity to store a list of all countries. We want this listing to be manageable by a user with proper permissions, so that it can be updated as they do business with new countries.

1. Open the solution, and navigate to the **Entities** tab.

2. Click on **New** to add a new entity to the solution.

3. Fill in the mandatory fields, and define where this entity will be visible. In our case, we will make this entity visible only in the **Settings** area. We are setting the **Ownership** of this entity to **Organization**, thus making it available across the environment.

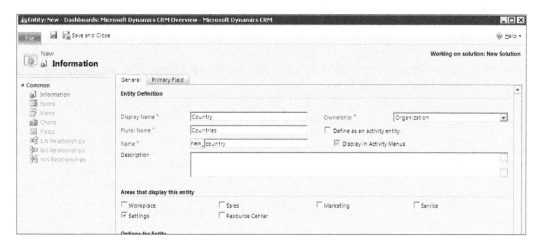

4. Additionally, the **Options for Entity** section allows you to define some of the standard elements and behaviors that can be included with the entity. These are comprised of behavioral settings, data settings, and configurations for mobile and Outlook. These settings give you a granular access to configure how an entity can interact with the system and other entities, what processes can be run against this entity, and storage options for related files.

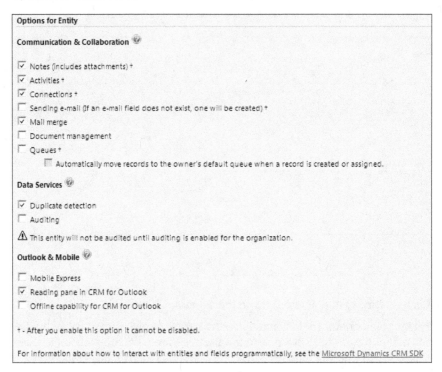

5. Before clicking on the **Save** icon, direct your attention to the second tab named **Primary Field**. All entities will need to have a primary field, and we can define the properties of such fields on this tab. We will define the display name as `Country`, leave the **Requirement Level** with the default value **Business Required**, and the **Type** as **Single Line of Text**.

6. Now we click on **Save**.

7. Once the entity is created, additional options to edit **Forms**, **Views**, **Fields**, and **Relationships** become available.

8. Great job! Now we have the entity created and we can start working with it.

Removing an entity that is not being used by our customization is again a relatively simple task.

1. In our solution package, select the entity.

2. Click on the **Delete** button.

 If the entity does not have any remaining associations with other entities in the system, it will be removed. Otherwise, a message will prompt you, and additional information is provided to help in identifying what relationships are preventing you from deleting this entity.

How it works...

Each entity is stored in the database as a set of two tables. The first one stores the base entity, while the second one stores the customizations to the entity. Creating a new entity in fact creates this set of tables, one that stores the entity generic properties, and another that stores each data fields defined. So, in our case, we will have a table called `new_countryBase`, and another called `new_countryExtensionBase`, as seen in the following two images:

```
dbo.new_countryBase
   Columns
      new_countryId (PK, uniqueidentifier, not n(
      CreatedOn (datetime, null)
      CreatedBy (uniqueidentifier, null)
      ModifiedOn (datetime, null)
      ModifiedBy (uniqueidentifier, null)
      CreatedOnBehalfBy (uniqueidentifier, null)
      ModifiedOnBehalfBy (uniqueidentifier, null)
      OrganizationId (FK, uniqueidentifier, null)
      statecode (int, not null)
      statuscode (int, null)
      VersionNumber (timestamp, null)
      ImportSequenceNumber (int, null)
      OverriddenCreatedOn (datetime, null)
      TimeZoneRuleVersionNumber (int, null)
      UTCConversionTimeZoneCode (int, null)
```

The extended table has the following definition:

This information is only available while working On-Premise. With a Dynamics CRM 2011 Online instance, there is no direct access to the database.

Making modifications directly to the database in Dynamics CRM 2011 is not supported. This can cause various issues. All data access should go through web services. When creating custom reports, use the views. They also present the trimmed data security.

See also

▸   Additional information related to entities can be found on TechNet at
    `http://technet.microsoft.com/en-us/library/gg309396.aspx`.

Creating and managing fields

Once we have an entity ready to work with, whether it's a new custom entity or an existing out-of-the-box entity, we can start managing the information to be captured.

Getting ready

In this recipe, we will be building on the custom **Country** entity we created in the previous recipe. Open the created solution and navigate to the created **Country** entity. We will be adding two more fields to capture the country code and display sequence.

How to do it...

In order to add the additional fields to capture information, we will follow these steps:

1. Expand the **Entities** section in the solution, and expand the **Country** custom entity that we created:

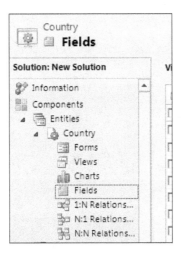

2. Select the **Forms** option, and look at the view of forms associated with this entity.

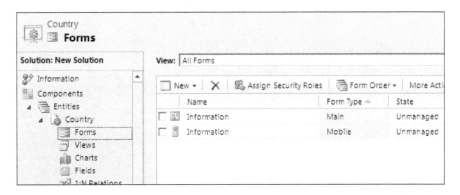

3. By default, we will be presented with two views, one that we will customize, and another mobile form. We will open the first form, of type **Main**.

4. From the bottom-right of the screen, we will click on the **New Field** button.

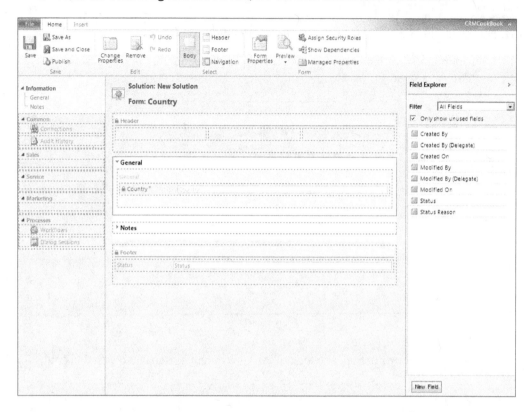

5. We will create a field with the display name of Country Code, no requirements constraint, and of type text, single line, with a maximum length of 3. We will be using this field to capture country codes such as CA, USA, and UK.

6. Once complete, we'll click on **Save and Close**. The new field will show in the listing of **All Fields** in **Field Explorer**.

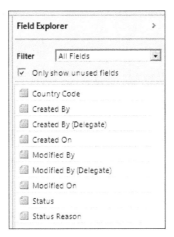

7. Now we can simply drag this field on the form, under our **Country** field.

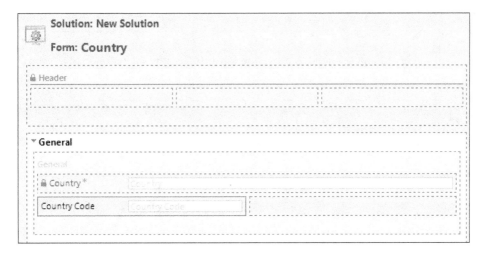

8. With this field already added to the form, we can add a new field called **Display Sequence**, of type **Whole Number**, as described by the following screenshot:

9. We will be adding this field to the same form. This entity will be used in the next recipe. The end result should look like the following image:

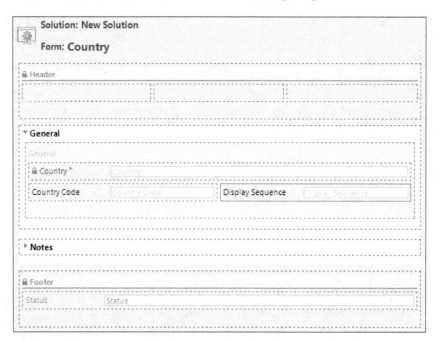

10. Now we can click **Save** on the form screen, and then **Publish**. All customizations must be published before they are visible to all users.

11. Once all customizations are published, we can verify the form by navigating to the **Settings** area, and looking under **Extensions**. We will find our custom **Countries** entity there.

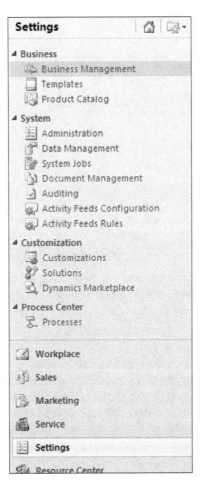

12. Clicking on **Countries** will show us a view of all **Active Countries** (default view). We can click on **New** to see how the customized form will look.

13. If we are not satisfied with the way the form looks, we can go back to the solution and tweak the look of it again, or else we can proceed further.

How it works...

Because we have configured the new entity to be visible only in the **Settings** section, we will have to navigate to **Settings** to get access to the listing of countries we will be adding to the system. We have customized it as such so that when we build a more complex solution later in the book, we can make sure that only authorized users will be able to see and modify the listing of all countries in such a way.

There's more...

Dynamics CRM 2011 allows us to define a large number of field types. We have only covered two simple examples here, one of text and one of whole numbers. Additional field types will be described in the following recipes, when we start looking at how to script these fields.

▶ For additional information on creating fields and adding them to forms, see the TechNet documentation at `http://technet.microsoft.com/en-us/library/gg334527`.

Creating and managing forms

In certain instances, we will require additional forms for the same entity. One obvious example is when we need to implement role-based forms. In such instances, a specific role could have access to only a subset of fields, while a different role could have access to other fields. We could have an overlap of fields available to all roles too.

Getting ready

Open the previously created solution, and navigate to the **Countries** entity we created. In the view of **All Forms**, by default, we only have the two forms, one for the normal use and one for mobile.

How to do it...

Adding a new form can be achieved as follows:

1. From the **All Forms** view, select **New | Main Form**, or simply click on **New**.

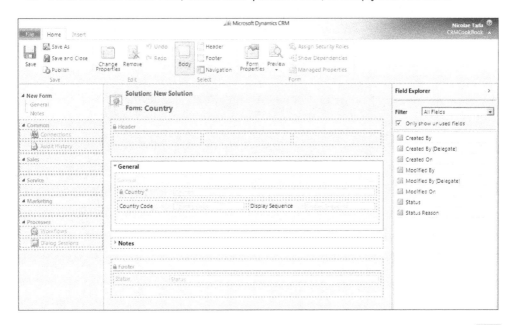

2. On this new form, we can remove the **Country Code** and **Display Sequence** fields, by selecting each field and clicking on **Remove** on the ribbon.

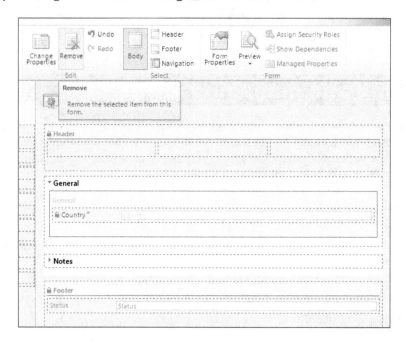

3. Click on the **Form Properties** button on the ribbon, and on the **Display** tab (second from the left) to define a new name for our form.

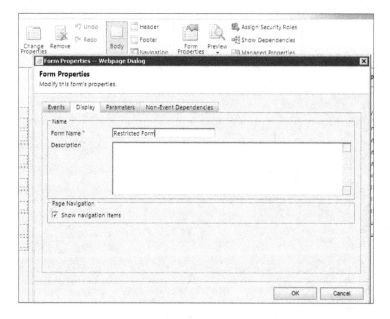

4. Once the fields are removed and the form renamed, we can save and publish the new form.

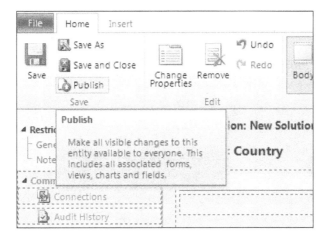

5. With the form published, we can verify the listing of **All Forms** to make sure the form is saved.

6. To verify how this form is presented to users, we can navigate to **Country** created in the system, and select from the available forms.

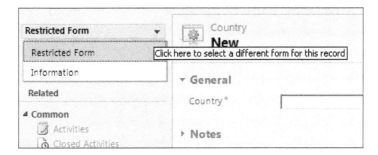

7. Now, both forms are available to be selected for users that have permissions to view both. We will be covering role-based forms later in a different recipe.

Removing a form is also a relatively simple process.

1. Navigate in the solution package to the **All Forms** view and select the form to be removed.

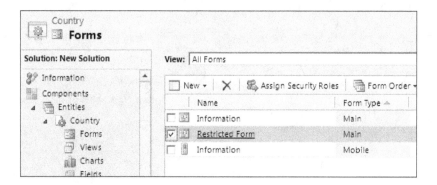

2. Click on the **Delete** button.
3. Publish all customizations.

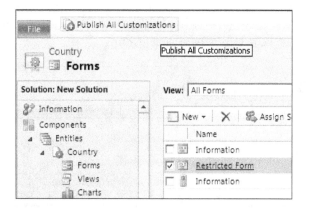

How it works...

Creating various forms for entities can help reduce the amount of scripting required to hide/show fields. We can assign specific forms to specific user roles, and thus reduce the amount of client-side processing on the form.

Creating and managing scripts

JavaScript scripts are added to a solution package just like any other resource. They are becoming part of the package, and thus are easily portable to other environments, along with the solution.

Getting ready

Using the existing solution package we have created, we will be adding a new JavaScript resource.

How to do it...

To add a new JavaScript resource, navigate to **Settings**, and open your existing solution package. Follow these steps to add a script resource:

1. In the package, navigate to **Web Resources**.

2. In the **Web Resources** view, select **New** to add a new script resource.

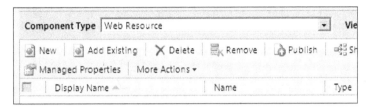

3. Give the resource a name, and select the Script (Jscript) option from the **Type** drop-down list. The **Display Name** should be in a readable format. It is good practice to always add a **Description** for other developers that will follow in your foot steps to easily identify the content of the library without having to open the file.

4. Click on **Save**, and then on **Publish**. Now you have a JavaScript resource added to your solution package. There is no actual script added yet, so let's do that.

5. Click on the **Text Editor** button. A new form will open allowing you to type in your script.

6. Click **OK**, then **Save** and **Publish** your resource again.

7. Now we have a script added as part of the solution package. It is not related to any action, but we will cover that in one of the later recipes.

Sometimes a script resource can become obsolete, and we would want to remove it. In order to remove a script resource that is not associated with any other system entities, perform the following steps:

1. From the **Web Resources** view, select the script.

2. Click on **Delete**.

3. Make sure to click on **Publish all Customizations** for the changes to take effect. Now your script resource has been removed.

Creating and managing other resources

JavaScript resources are not the only available resource that can be added to your solution package. Other file types can be also associated in a similar manner, including HTML pages, stylesheets, image files, as well as Silverlight controls.

Getting ready

Navigate to your solution package, and expand the **Web Resources** section.

How to do it...

On the **Web Resources** view, follow these steps:

1. Click on **New** to add a new resource.
2. In the new window, give the resource a name, a display name, and add a description if necessary.
3. Select **JPG** for **Type** as we will be adding an image resource.

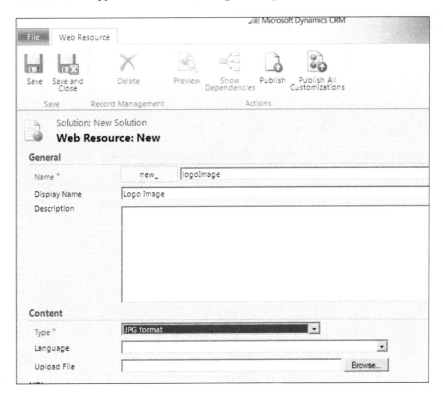

4. Click on **Browse** to retrieve a locally-stored image.

5. Once the picture is selected, click on **Save** and then on **Publish**. Now your resource is added to the solution package.

> The **URL** field shows a reference to how you access the resource image directly. We will be using part of that URL in scripts where we work with image resources.

Creating and managing workflows

Workflows, along with the newly introduced concept of dialogs have all been grouped as **Process in Dynamics CRM 2011**. The workflow concept remains similar to that of previous versions, with some additional functionality.

Getting ready

We will be adding a very basic workflow to our existing solution package. Open the already created solution package to work with.

How to do it...

In order to add a new workflow using the wizard, perform the following steps:

1. In the solution package, navigate to **Processes** and open the **Processes** view.

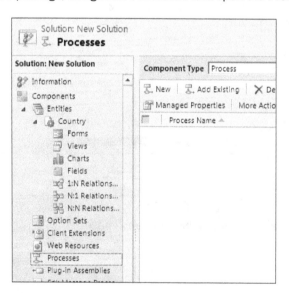

2. Click on **New** to create a new workflow.

3. On the **Process: New** page, give the new workflow a name, select an entity it will work against, and from the **Category** drop-down, select **Workflow**.

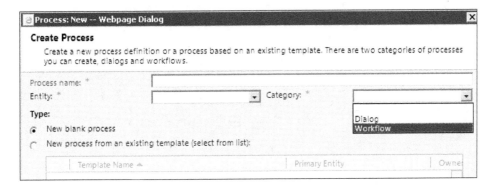

4. Leave default the selection for **New blank process**, and click on the **OK** button.

5. The process wizard starts, and it allows us to configure the workflow properties and parameters.

6. In the **Options for Automatic Processes** section, I will select the scope to be **Organization**, and the start to be generated by the **Record is created** event.

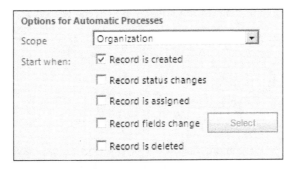

7. Next, we will add a simple e-mail notification step to be executed. Click on **Add Step**, and select **Send E-mail**. This will add the **Send e-mail** step, and allows us to configure the properties.

8. Click on **Set Properties**, and start customizing the e-mail properties. We can add the **From** to be the current user that creates the record, and the **To** field to be the owner of the record. Also, we can create a subject and body.

9. Click on **Save and Close** to complete the message configuration.

10. Additionally, you can define a step description in the workflow step wizard window.

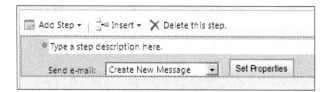

11. With our step created and configured properly, now we can save the workflow. Click on **Save**. In order to enable this workflow, we have to activate it. Click next on **Activate**.

12. Click **OK** on the **Process Activation Confirmation** window. If there is no error in the workflow, it will become active.

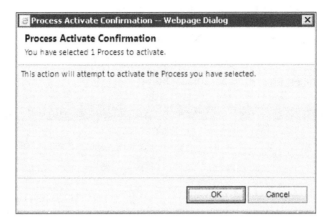

13. Once the workflow is activated, we can create a new record and verify that it performs as expected.

How it works...

This sample workflow we created sends an e-mail confirmation once a new **Contact** record is created. As long as the workflow stays active in the system, it will execute on each record creation, as configured. Other configuration options include the capture of field value changes, new assignment of record to another user, or on record deletion. The record deletion event captured can also be used to validate record deletion, and stop the process if certain conditions are not met.

See also

 ▸ For additional information on Processes, including workflows and dialogs, as well as a comparison between the two, see the TechNet articles at `http://technet. microsoft.com/en-us/library/gg309471.aspx`.

Creating and managing dialogs

A dialog differs from a workflow through the fact that it is an interactive process, where user input is required. The addition of dialogs offers new possibilities with Dynamics CRM 2011.

Getting ready

We will be using the same solution package we created earlier.

How to do it...

Adding a dialog is done by performing the following steps:

1. Open the existing solution package, and navigate to **Processes**.

2. In the **Processes** view, click on **New** to add a new process.

3. On the **Process: New** window, select **Dialog** this time.

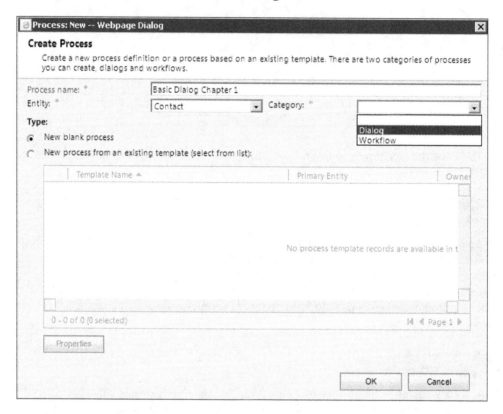

4. Keep **New blank process** selected and click on **OK**.

5. The dialog configuration window allows us configure the dialog details. A dialog can be started as either an on-demand process, or as a child of another process. This allows us to create smaller dialogs, and chain them together as required to achieve our final result. We will mark this dialog as an on-demand process, so we can see the very basic functionality available.

6. To capture user interaction, we will first add a page to the dialog, and then a **Prompt and Response** on that page.

7. Click on **Set Properties** to define the prompt and available answers.

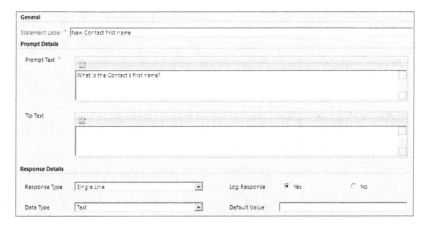

8. Click on **Save and Close** to finish defining this step.

9. In the process builder, add a new **Update** step that will fill in the captured details within the form field.

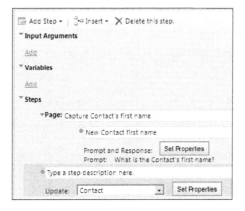

10. Click on **Set Properties** to define which value gets assigned to what field. We are being presented with the standard **Contact** form. Click into the **First Name** field, and from the **Form Assistant**, select **New contact first name** under **Local Values** in the **Look for** drop-down list, and **Response Text**. Click on **Add** and then **OK**.

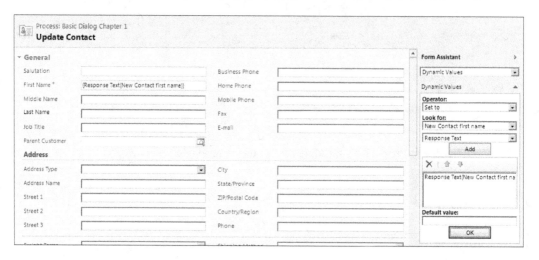

11. **Save and Close** this form. Save the dialog and activate it.

12. To test this newly created dialog, create a new **Contact** record, and from the ribbon, click on the **Start Dialog** button.

13. From the selection window that opens up, select the dialog we created earlier.

14. Click on **OK** and answer the prompt question.

15. Click on **Next**. When the dialog finishes, an end of dialog window is displayed. Click on **Finish**.

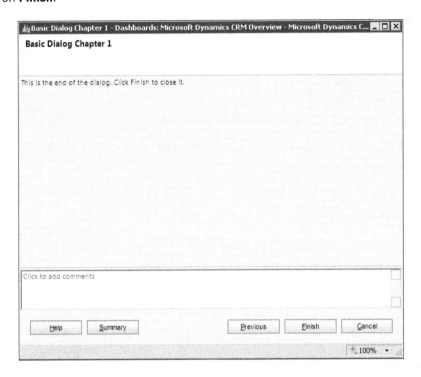

16. Once the dialog completes execution, you will see the value captured during the dialog populated into the contact's first name field.

How it works...

For demonstration purposes we have only captured the contact's first name and populated the first name field. More steps can be added to a dialog to capture additional information and guide a system user in capturing all required details through a dialog rather than by using a free form. This way a "script" can be created for the user to capture information in a specific order, thus enforcing a clean, repeatable process in dealing with customers in a Call Centre scenario.

Starting a workflow from a dialog

We have looked at workflows and dialogs. But they can function together to achieve a result. For example, we can start from a dialog, capture specific information, and then kick off a workflow as part of the same process to process the information and generate a result.

Getting ready

Using the same solution package, we will be creating two new processes. One is a workflow that sends an e-mail when a field value changes, which we will mark as a child process. The other is a dialog that will call this workflow.

How to do it...

Create the child workflow by performing the following steps:

1. Create a new workflow, on the **Account** entity this time. Mark it to run as a child process.

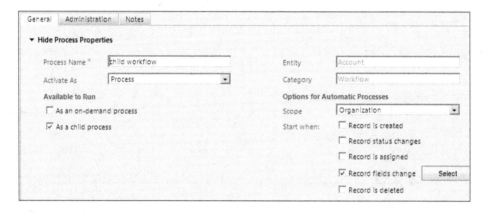

2. Add a send e-mail step to the workflow, and configure the email properties as described in a previous recipe.

3. Activate the workflow.

Create the parent dialog that will kick-of this workflow by performing the following steps:

1. Create the parent dialog on the same entity, as a dialog.

2. Create a new page, then a question with a Yes/No option set. Create a new check condition step, in which if the value selected in the dialog is **Yes**, then create a **Start Child Workflow** step. Look up the child workflow we created earlier and select it.

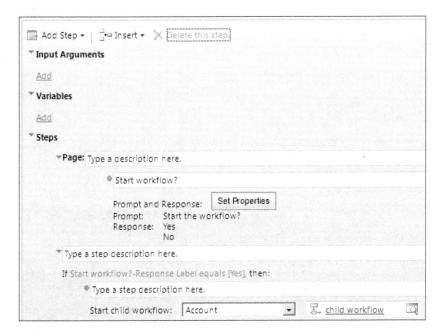

3. Save and activate this dialog.

How it works...

The dialog we have created, as simple as it is, prompts the user to decide whether they want to run a workflow or not. When the user selects **Yes**, the workflow is started.

We can easily test this functionality by going to a new account, and selecting from the ribbon the **Start Dialog** button. A window prompts us to select the dialog we will run.

We can easily check the execution status of both the dialog and the workflow by navigating on the account to the **Processes** section.

These two views will give us details about the processes that run against the current account, and the status of each.

Working with security roles and permissions

Security roles and permission can be configured as part of the same solution package. This allows us to port these configurations from one environment to another. Be aware though that there are some limitations in the use of security roles as part of a solution. One of the most important is a limitation where roles can only be configured at a top business unit when they are saved as part of a solution package.

Getting ready

We will be working within the same solution package we created earlier.

How to do it...

In order to add a new security role we must perform the following steps:

1. Open the existing solution package.
2. Navigate to the **Security Roles** view.

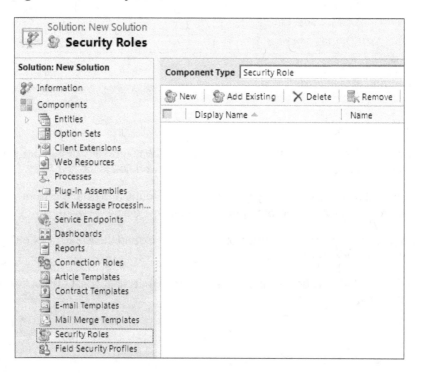

3. To create a completely new role, select **New**. A better approach is to modify one of the existing roles by selecting **Add Existing**, but for the purpose of this recipe we will create a new role. Click on **New**.

4. Give the role a name and make the necessary modifications. Click **Save and Close**. The new role is added as part of the solution.

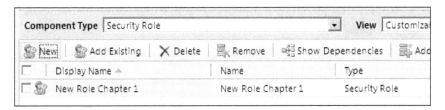

5. With this new role created, we can go back to the custom **Country** form we previously created. Open the form and click on **Assign Security Roles**.

6. Deselect the selected security roles, and select the newly created security role.

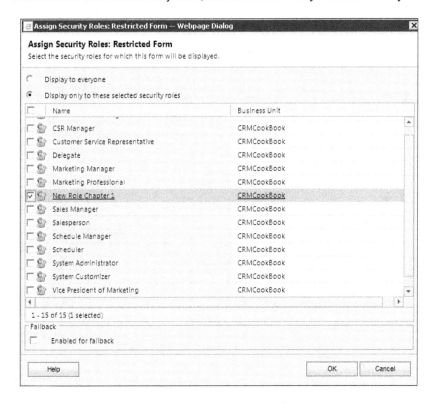

7. Click on **OK**, save changes, and publish all customizations.

How it works...

At this point we have a new security role added to the solution package. Additionally, we have configured the custom **Country** form to be visible only by users that are assigned the newly created security role.

See also

▸   For additional details on working with security roles, read the TechNet articles at `http://technet.microsoft.com/en-us/library/gg334717.aspx`.

2
Scripting Form Fields

In this chapter, we will cover the following:

- ▸ Working with text fields
- ▸ Working with number fields
- ▸ Working with currency fields
- ▸ Working with date and time fields
- ▸ Working with option sets
- ▸ Working with lookups

Introduction

In this chapter, we will focus on a few short examples of using JavaScript to interact with various types of form fields.

The recipes will be using the same environment that we provisioned in the previous chapter, but you can use any environment you have available, presuming you have permissions to customize forms. None of the recipes in this chapter are based on the configuration built in *Chapter 1, Overview of Dynamics CRM 2011 Customization*.

Working with text fields

In this recipe, we will be retrieving information from the Phone field of a Contact entity. We can work in the same fashion with any other default text fields on any entity form, or with custom fields.

Getting ready

If you have a solution created from the previous chapter, open that solution. If not, create a new solution package. We will be saving all configurations as part of a solution package.

How to do it...

In order to associate our script with a field on the **Contact** form, we will follow these steps:

1. Navigate to **Settings | Solutions**.

2. Open the previously created solution package or create a new one.

3. Select **Entities**, and click on **Add Existing** to add the **Contact** entity, as shown in the following screenshot:

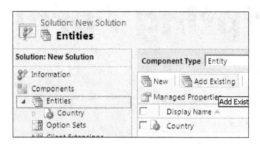

4. Scroll down until you find **Contact** and select it. Then, click on **OK**, as shown in the following screenshot:

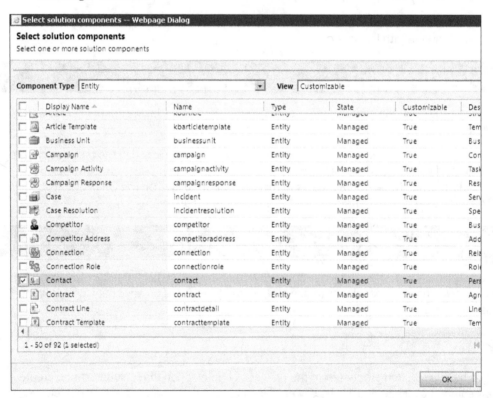

5. Now your solution will include customization options for **Contact**:

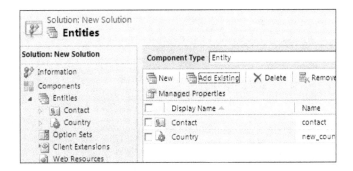

6. Click on **Web Resources** and add a new JScript resource. We will name it **JSContact**, as shown in the following screenshot:

7. Save and publish, then close the window.

8. Expand **Contact** and select **Forms**. Open the default **Information** main form by double-clicking on it.

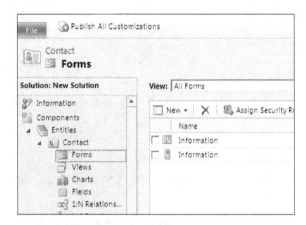

9. Double-click on the business phone field. We will be adding a script to the OnChange event of this field. The script will execute when the focus is moved off this field. This functionality is similar to capturing the OnBlur standard JavaScript form event.

10. On the **Field Properties** window, select the **Events** tab at the top.

11. In the **Event List** section, expand **Form Libraries**, and add the previously added JavaScript resource, as shown in the following screenshot:

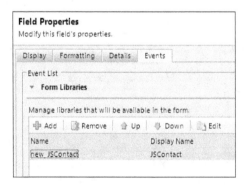

12. In the Event Handlers section, make sure the selected event is `OnChange`, and add a new function named **ReadBusinessPhone**. Make sure the enabled checkbox is selected, then click on **OK**

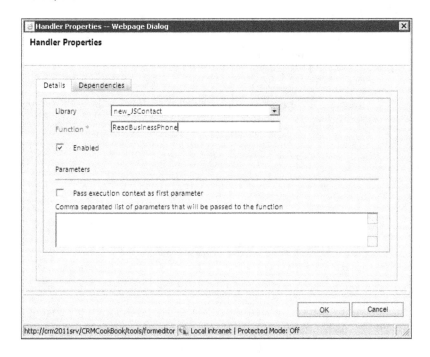

13. Click on **OK** again to close the **Field Properties** window.

14. Save and publish the **Contact** form, and then close it.

15. Before we can test this, we have to add the JavaScript function that will be executed to our web resource we have referenced. Let's go back to our solution package, to **Web Resource**, and double-click on the **JSContact** resource.

16. In the window that opens, click on the **Text Editor** button. Alternatively, if we have created the JavaScript resource in another text editor, we can just browse to it and load it. It will override the existing file, so be careful not override other functions in the same resource.

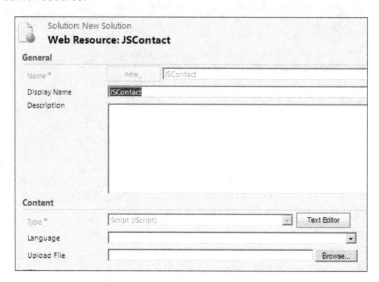

17. Add the following code to your resource. Pay close attention to the casing, as JavaScript is case sensitive.

```
function ReadBusinessPhone()
{
    var myBusinessPhone;
    myBusinessPhone = Xrm.Page.getAttribute("telephone1").
getValue();
    alert("You have entered: " + myBusinessPhone);
}
```

18. Save and publish your resource, then close the **Edit Content** window.

19. Save the solution, and then close it.

20. Now you can test your script. The end result should be similar to the following screenshot:

How it works...

While our sample script does not really do much other than retrieve the input and return it in a pop-up window, from here on you can do more complex things, such as formatting and validation. Those are standard JavaScript string operations in most cases.

There's more...

Once you have the value of the text field captured in your script, you can do more interesting processing. The following examples describe some of the common actions I use on regular basis.

Retrieving the field name to be used in the script

Looking at the **Field** properties, as described in step 10, if we open the **Details** tab, the **Name** field holds the actual field name we have to use in JavaScript:

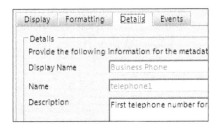

Formatting phone numbers

One common formatting I implement on all phone number fields is the formatting of the number. In order to make it readable and user friendly, we can check to make sure the length is either 10 or 11 characters, and then format it for North America in the following way:

+1-XXX-XXX-XXXX

Remove "-" before the count to make sure you are getting the correct length, and also check that all input is numeric.

Validating Country/Region against State/Province relationship

Another common validation that can be implemented is the validation of **Country/Region** versus **State/Province**. Out of the box, the **State/Province** field comes before the **Country/ Region** field, so we can read the value in **State/Province**, and based on that prepopulate the **Country** value.

Writing information back to the text field

Once we have processed the value retrieved from the text field, we can write it back to the same or another text field. The line of code to do so is as follows:

```
Xrm.Page.getAttribute("telephone1").setValue(myBusinessPhone);
```

This assumes that we will be writing the information to a field named **telephone1**, and the variable that stores the processed string is named `myBusinessPhone`.

Working with number fields

In this chapter, we will be working with a variation of the text field, and the number fields. By default, Dynamics CRM allows us a few fields with various number formats and data types associated.

The following field types are standard in Dynamics CRM:

- **Whole Number** – this format includes values from -2,147,483,648 to 2,147,483,647 on the default format of **None**. Additional formats include the following:
  - **Duration** – this is a drop-down list box with values in minutes, hours and days
  - **Time Zone** – this is a drop-down list box with time zone options
  - **Language** – this is a drop-down list box of available languages for the user
- **Floating Point Number** – this format includes values from 0 to 1,000,000,000 and the precision can be configured anywhere from 0 to 5 decimal places.
- **Decimal Number** – while this format includes the same range of values as the floating point number, the precision can be configured from 0 to 10 decimal places.

Addressing these field types in script uses the same syntax, but we have to be aware of how we initially define them, as the data type cannot be changed after creation.

> The only way to change the data type defined for a field is to remove the field from the form, publish the form, and then remove the field from the entity and republish it. Afterwards we can recreate the required field with the updated data type. Pay close attention when taking this approach, as trying to re-import the managed solution after this change will fail. The reason for this is that you are trying to do exactly what you were prevented from doing in the first place.

Getting ready

Open the solution from the previous recipe if not already opened. We will use the same solution package to store this new customization.

The client-side scripting is the same for these field types, and JavaScript will handle automatically the data type of the value we are reading.

How to do it...

In order to work with a number field follow these steps:

1. Create a new form field, named `new_number` of type **Whole Number**, of default format **None**. Add it to the form.

2. Add a new JScript resource named `JSNumbers.js`.

3. Insert the following code:

```
function ReadNumberField()
{
    var myNumber;
    myNumber = Xrm.Page.getAttribute("new_number").getValue();
    alert("The number in the field is: " + myNumber);
}
```

4. Save and publish the resource.

5. Attach the function to the `OnChange` event of the field. Save and publish the form again.

6. Run the form and change the value in the field to **100**. You should be getting the following popup:

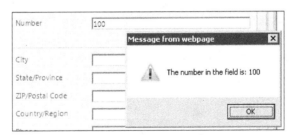

Reading a value from a number field is identical to reading a value from any other regular text field.

The difference between these fields is in the data that we can push back in this field, for example, if we try the following code to add a text value to a field defined as a Whole Number:

```
try
{
 Xrm.Page.getAtribute("new_number").setValue("AAA");
}
    catch(err)
{
    alert("Error: " + err.message);
}
```

Working with currency

Defining fields as currency allows proper visual formatting for a better user experience. Adding the field give us an option to define the currency precision, as well as maximum and minimum values to delimit the range.

Getting ready

We will reuse the solution from the *Working with number fields* recipe. Open it, if not already opened.

How to do it...

1. Open up the **Contact** form we have used previously, and add a new field named **Currency Field** (new_currencyfield) to that form. Let's define our currency field with a precision of 2, and set minimum value to 0.00 and maximum value to 1,000,000.00.

2. Add a new JScript resource named new_JSCurrency.

3. First off, we will create a function to retrieve the value of the current field, once we change it. We attach our function to the OnChange event of the field. The function will look as follows:

```
function ReadCurrency()
{
        var myCurrencyField;
        myCurrencyField = Xrm.Page.getAttribute("new_
currencyfield").getValue();
        alert("The value of this Currency field is: " +
myCurrencyField);
}
```

Here we are basically reading the field value into our variable `myCurrencyField`, and displaying it in a popup as follows:

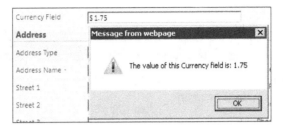

How it works...

A few things are important to note here. First off, the currency is visually formatted on the screen, adding the "$" symbol, while the database end only stores the actual float value.

Additionally, if you look at the fields generated on the form, all currency fields are accompanied by a base currency field in the system.

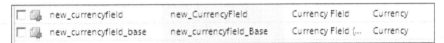

The base currency is a conversion to the default system currency. Users are allowed to use their own region's currency as long as it is made available in the system, but the system converts the currency based on the conversion rate of this value to the base currency (the default system currency).

Be careful which currency field you use when generating reports. You have a choice to use the either the regular currency field, or the base currency field, depending on the scope of the report.

There's more...

While we can write back to a field defined as `Currency` the same way we write to a regular text field, a little bit of validation goes a long way. Using the standard JavaScript parsing function adds another check point. The following block of code describes the process to populate our currency field with a value of 1.25:

```
function WriteCurrency()
{
    var myCurrencyValue = 6.25;
    Xrm.Page.getAttribute("new_currencyfield").setValue(parseFloat(myC
urrencyValue));
}
```

This time let's add this function to the form `OnLoad` event. Now every time we open a **Contact** form the value of our `Currency` field will get updated to 6.25, and we will get a popup when we change it.

Working with date and time

Defining a field as **Date and Time** allows an optimized data input, by presenting a floating calendar and capturing the user selection.

When creating a **Date and Time** field, you have a choice to specify whether to capture the date and time, or just the date.

Getting ready

For the purpose of this recipe, we will be building within the scope of the previously created solution. We will use the existing **Birthday** field on the **Contact** form, and target our scripts to this field. This field is defined as `Date Only`.

How to do it...

We will be building a new function to read the value from this field first. Follow these steps:

1. Add a new JScript web resource, named `JSDateTime` (`new_JSDateTime`).

2. Insert the following function which reads the current field value and pops up an alert with the value:

```
function ReadBirthday()
{
        var myContactBirthday;
        myContactBirthday = Xrm.Page.getAttribute("birthdate").
getValue();
        alert("Contact birthday is: " + myContactBirthday);
}
```

3. Associate this function with the `OnChange` event of the **Birthday** field on the **Contact** form.

4. Save and Publish.

5. Open a contact and change the **Birthday** field value. A popup will come up looking as follows:

How it works...

One thing to note about the **Date and Time** fields in Dynamics CRM is that, even though we define a field as Date Only, the full date and time is stored, with a time defaulted to 0. If we want to retrieve only the date, we can either use the standard JavaScript functions to extract the year, month and day from the Date object as follows:

```
var year = myContactBirthday.getFullYear();
var month = myContactBirthday.getMonth(); // from 0 to 11
var day = myContactBirthday.getDate(); // from 1 to 31
month = month + 1;
alert("Year: " + year + ", Month: " + month + ", Day: " + day);
```

There's more...

On a new field defined as either **Date Only** or **Date and Time**, the following code will add the current date:

```
function SetBirthday()
{
    var currentDateTime = new Date();
    Xrm.Page.getAttribute("new_myDate").setValue(currentDateTime);
}
```

Additionally, if a specific date value has to be added, it can be defined with standard JavaScript functionality in the variable that is being passed on to the `setValue` function.

Working with option sets

Starting with option sets, things get a little bit more interesting. Now we are talking about a set of values stored in a structure similar to a dictionary's collection of name/value pairs.

Getting ready

We will be using the previously created solution. Open the solution if not already opened. Alternatively, you can create a brand new solution and add the **Contact** entity to your solution.

How to do it...

In order to work with an option set, let's follow these steps:

1. Open the **Contact** entity added to the solution package.

2. Open the main form.

3. Add a new field defined as **option set**. We will define this field as not using an existing option set, and no default value.

4. Let's add the following values:

   ❑ Example A, Value 100,000,000

   ❑ Example B, Value 100,000,001

   ❑ Example C, Value 100,000,002

5. Add a new JScript resource named JSOptionSet (new_JSOptionSet)

6. Add the following function that reads the selected value of the option set and displays it in an alert window:

```
function GetOSValue()
{
    var sval = Xrm.Page.getAttribute("new_optionset").
getSelectedOption().text;
    alert("Selected value: " + sval);
}
```

7. Back on the form, associate the function with the OnChange event of the newly created **option set** field.

8. Save and publish.

9. Open a contact and change the **option set** value. The following alert should be seen:

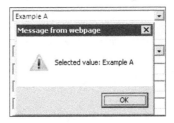

How it works...

Our function selects the option set element on the form, retrieves the selected value, and pulls the `label` property of the selected option. Alternatively the value can be retrieved if necessary by using the following line of code:

```
var sval = Xrm.Page.getAttribute("new_optionset").
getSelectedOption().value;
```

There's more...

Reading the selected value of an option set and acting on it is only the first part. How do you set a value of an option set programmatically as a result of another element on the form changing?

Assigning a value programmatically

When we need to assign a value to an option set programmatically, we need to use the `Value` defined, not the `Label`. So what do we do, start memorizing and hardcoding these numbers?

One alternative is to build a small helper function that allows us to loop through the values of the option set, and identify the value based on the label we are providing. Such a function could look as follows:

```
function SetOSValue(osName, osLabel)
{
    var options = Xrm.Page.getAttribute(osName).getOptions();
    for(i = 0; i < options.length; i++)
    {
        if (options[i].text == osLabel)
        Xrm.Page.getAttribute(osName).setValue(options[i].value);
    }
}
```

Once we find a match on the label we can assign the value retrieved directly from the system. This will also handle cases where certain values could be updated accidentally.

We can use this helper function in the context of our recipe by creating a new function, and associating it to the `OnLoad` event of the form. All we do here is call the helper function, passing as parameters the name of the option set, and the value we want to set as default.

```
function SetMe()
{
    SetOSValue("new_optionset","Example C");
}
```

Working with lookups

Working with lookups presents a new set of challenges. In a lookup we are basically pointing to existing values populated in another entity. We are looking for the ID of the target selected entity.

 Be aware that once values are loaded into an environment, ID's are automatically associated. If you move your solution to another environment and reload the source entity data, new ID's are being generated, and you will have to update your script as such.

Getting ready

For the purpose of this recipe we will be using the existing solution we have already created. If you have not created a solution already, now is a good time to do so.

Add to your solution the **Contact** entity. We've been focusing on making changes to this entity, and this recipe will follow that same pattern. Note that you can do this with any system entity, whether out of the box or custom.

How to do it...

In order to read the selected value in a lookup, follow these steps:

1. Create a new custom entity called **State**.
2. Configure the **Ownership** to **Organization** so it is readily available to all users.
3. For **Areas that display this entity**, select **Settings** only. We do not want any users having direct access to this entity, but we want them to reference it only on the **Contact** forms.

4. In the **Options for Entity** area, uncheck **Notes** as we do not want to have a **Notes** field associated. Your entity definition form should look as follows:

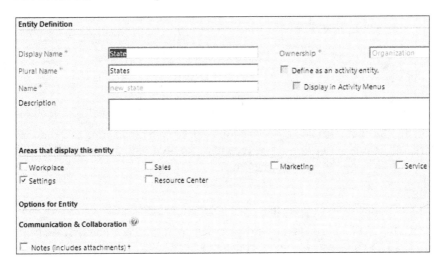

5. Save your new entity.

6. Once saved, open up the main form to configure it.

7. Change the label of the **Name** field to State by double-clicking on the field and changing the **Label** on the **Display** tab.

8. Add a new State Code text field to the form.

9. Add a new Order field of type Whole Number to the form, with no format and a start value of 0.

10. Save and publish your new entity. Once you refresh the browser window, in the **Settings** area your new entity should display as follows:

11. Open up the **States** extensions and let's start adding some sample data. The form looks as follows:

12. Once we have a few sample data records, we are ready to create our lookups.

13. On the **Contact** form add a new lookup field. We will be pointing to the previously created **States** entity. Select the **Type** to be **Lookup**, and the **Target Record Type** to be **State**. Add the field to the form.

14. Save and publish.

15. Create a new JScript resource in your solution, named JSLookup (new_JSLookup).

16. Add a function that reads the selected value in our newly created **State** field, and displays it in an alert. The script could look as follows:

```
function ReadState()
{
    var state = new Array();
    state = Xrm.Page.getAttribute("new_state").getValue();
    if(state != null)
    {
        var stateText = state[0].name;
        var stateId = state[0].id;
        var stateType = state[0].entityType;

        alert("State is: " + stateText + ", ID: " + stateId + "
of type: " + stateType);
    }
}
```

17. Do note that in our code we always check to make sure a value was indeed selected before we retrieve the properties.

18. The name returns the actual text we see in the lookup, the ID returns the internal ID of the selection and the entityType returns the type used. Note that the ID is what we will need later on when I show you how to programmatically populate this field.

19. Once we open the **Contact** form and we change the **State** field value, a popup will give us all the details about the selection we have made.

How it works...

In order to retrieve the selection in a lookup, we create an array to store the returned values. As a lookup only holds a single selection value, the result will be a single element array, with the element at index 0.

One important aspect is, we always have to check and make sure that we have indeed a value returned in the array, otherwise we will get an error when trying to read the value at that index and there is nothing there. For this reason we are checking if the array is not null before reading the value.

There's more...

While reading the value selected in a lookup constitutes one step, many times we need to push a value back into a lookup, either to clear it or to define a new selection on the form.

Clearing a lookup selection

For us to clear a lookup, all we need to do is set its value to null. The following script does just that:

```
function ClearState()
{
    var state = Xrm.Page.getAttribute("new_state");
    if (state != null)
    {
     Xrm.Page.getAttribute("new_state").setValue(null);
    }
}
```

Associate this function with the `OnLoad` event of the form, so that every time we open a contact, the **State** field gets cleared.

Changing a lookup selection

There are circumstances when you want a certain lookup value to be programmatically assigned based on some other action on the form. This is relatively easy to achieve once you have identified the IDs of the values available.

Instead of assigning a null value like we did in the previous example, we have to build our input as demonstrated in the following function:

```
function SetStateToNY()
{
     var state = new Array();
     state[0] = new Object();
     state[0].id = "{BA0762E4-64D2-E111-909E-00155D6C871A}";
     state[0].name = "New York";
     state[0].entityType = "new_state";

     Xrm.Page.getAttribute("new_state").setValue(state);
}
```

Be aware that if your ID assigned does not map to the ID in the system, it will appear to process correctly, adding the value to the lookup, but when you try to save your form, the following message appears:

Downloading the example code

You can download the example code files for all Packt books you have purchased from your account at http://www.packtpub.com . If you purchased this book elsewhere, you can visit http://www.packtpub.com/support and register to have the files e-mailed directly to you.

Expanding on the State example

Out of the box, Dynamics CRM allows the users to type any values in both the Country/Region and the State/Province fields. But oftentimes, we do not want to users to type and possibly misspell. For this reason we can implement filtered lookups in such way that once a Country is selected, the State/Province shows a trimmed-down list of only values relevant to that particular country.

In order not to break any internal functionality of CRM, including any pre-existing reports, we can still use the out of the box fields, but we'll put a different spin on it. Once a value is selected in the lookup, we can programmatically read that value, and assign it to the default text field. Also, we hide these default text fields so they don't overcrowd our form.

To take one step further, we can add an "Other" option to both Country and State lookups. When this value is selected, we can display the hidden fields allowing the user to type a value that is not already in the system.

The code could look similar to the following:

```
function setOTBState()
{
        var state = new Array();
        state = Xrm.Page.getAttribute("new_state").getValue();
        if(state != null)
        {
                var stateText = state[0].name;

                if(stateText != "Other")
                {
                        Xrm.Page.getAttribute("address1_stateorprovince").
setValue(stateText);
                        Xrm.Page.ui.controls.get("address1_
stateorprovince").setVisible(false);
                }
                else
                {
                        Xrm.Page.getAttribute("address1_stateorprovince").
setValue("");
                        Xrm.Page.ui.controls.get("address1_
stateorprovince").setVisible(true);
                }
        }
}
```

The new lines of code added in this example show you how to set a field as visible or hide it on a form.

3
Field Validation

In this chapter, we will cover:

- ▶ Custom e-mail field validation
- ▶ Custom web address field validation
- ▶ Validating the ticker symbol field
- ▶ Formatting phone numbers
- ▶ Formatting postal codes
- ▶ Replacing the Country and Province fields with lookups

Introduction

In this chapter, we will delve deeper into standard field formatting and validation. We will be looking at some of the most common scenarios.

Custom e-mail field validation

Working with e-mail fields has been greatly simplified. For the most part, we can just define the field as e-mail and, lo and behold, we need no customization and formatting.

There are exceptional cases to this. We might want to capture multiple e-mail fields, or validate other types of fields that are not defined as e-mail. For this purpose, we still need to pull out our JavaScript toolbox and draft some quick snippets of script. So let's get started.

Getting ready

By now we should have an environment created and proper permissions to tinker around with some customizations. Ideally we should have the permissions of a system customizer or a system administrator, or a similar custom role.

How to do it...

Generating a new e-mail field on a form using the simplistic UI wizard can easily be achieved by performing the following steps:

1. Open an existing solution, or create a new one.

2. Add the **Contact** entity to the solution, if not already added.

3. Open the main information form for editing.

4. Click on **New Field** to add a new e-mail field.

5. Name the field `Other e-Mail`, set the **Type** as **Single Line of Text**, and for **Format** select **E-mail**.

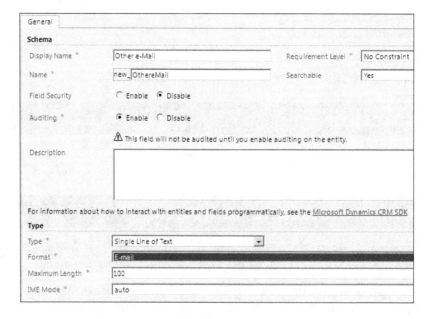

6. Add the field to the form, **Save** and **Publish** your form.

This approach adds an e-mail field to your form with the required validation. On change, the input is verified to map to a valid e-mail address format. Additionally, once a correct e-mail is entered, it is presented back to the user as a mailto hyperlink.

One disadvantage of the e-mail field validation built is the actual format validation. While the validation formula does check for a valid block of letters, followed by the @ symbol and another block of letters, it fails to check for an extension. Thus, we can easily end up with e-mail addresses formatted like demo@demo instead of a proper demo@demo.com.

For cases where we need to validate a proper e-mail address with a **Fully Qualified Domain Name** (**FQDN**) or if we need to accept only e-mail addresses from a specific domain, the following block of JavaScript code can come to the rescue:

```
function checkEmail(emailField)
{
    var email=/^([a-zA-Z0-9_.-])+@([a-zA-Z0-9_.-])+\.([a-zA-Z])+([a-zA-Z])+/;
    if(email.test(emailField))
    {
        // alert("true");
        return true;
    }
}
```

We are using regular expressions to define the mapping format for an e-mail address.

How it works...

The checkEmail() function we have just presented is meant to be used as a generic function we can call for any field we need to validate as e-mail. In order to validate the field we have just created we can create a new function, retrieve the value of the field, and pass it into our function. For reading from a single-line text field, refer to the respective recipe earlier in this book.

Once we define the regular expression, we can test the string from the user input against the expressions. If we have a match, we can raise an alert (commented out in our script with the // symbol, and then we can return true. The calling function can then process based on the return value.

There's more...

One other case when dealing with e-mail addresses is a situation where either a single or multiline text field is meant to capture a listing of e-mail addresses separated by a key symbol. Let's define the separation symbol as a comma.

The way to validate the input in such a case is by reading the whole input, separating the individual e-mail addresses, loading them in an array, then running our check against each one using the same checkEmail() function.

Assuming inputField is a string holding the user input, the following function will split the string, load the array, and run the check.

```
function checkInput(inputField)
{
  var flag = true;
  var emailArray = inputField.split(",");
  for(var i = 0; i < emailArray.length; i++)
  {
    if(!checkEmail(emailArray[i]))
    {
      flag = false;
      break;
    }
  }
  return flag;
}
```

Handling erroneous input

There are a few tricks that enable us to handle erroneous input from the user. First off, we want to display a message back to the user, to let him/her know what is wrong with the input they provided and why we are rejecting it. This can be easily achieved using a simple alert.

```
alert("You have entered an incorrect email address!");
```

Of course, you can be as creative as you want with the message you are passing back to the application user.

The other thing you might want to do is set the focus back on the field. You can achieve this with the following lines of code:

```
var field = Xrm.Page.ui.controls.get("fieldName");
field.setFocus();
```

While the first line gets a reference to the control, the second line actually sets the focus on it.

See also

- For more details on the `Xrm.Page` object model, refer to the MSDN documentation at `http://msdn.microsoft.com/en-us/library/gg328474.aspx`.
- For field datatype descriptions, check out the Dynamics CRM documentation at `http://rc.crm.dynamics.com/rc/2011/en-us/online/5.0/Help/ug_cust_entity_fields.htm`.

Custom web address field validation

URL fields are simply glorified text fields. Formatting is applied to these to generate the URL into a link format. Additionally, some minimal validation is applied, and the prefix `"http://"` is applied automatically if missing.

From a customization point of view, there isn't really that much that can be done with these fields, other than use them, as such.

In some circumstances we will want to make sure that the URL captured follows a specific set of business rules. As one example, we may expect to capture a link to a specific social network in which we can validate that input, and reject it if it does not conform.

Getting ready

Let's use for this example the same environment we created earlier. If you have jumped straight to this recipe, you can use any environment you have available, assuming you have the proper permissions to apply customizations, or you can create a new environment as described in the first chapter.

How to do it...

Perform the following steps to customize your solution:

1. Open an existing solution, or create a new one if one is not available.
2. Add the **Contact** entity to your solution, if not already added.

3. Add a new **Single Line of Text** field, name it LinkedIn, and set it to the **Format** of **URL**.

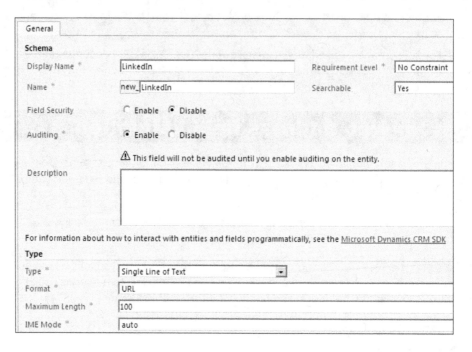

4. Add it to your form.

5. Generate a new JScript web resource file, named new_JSLinkedIn.

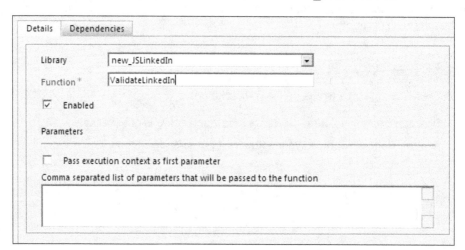

6. Add the following function:

```
function ValidateLinkedIn()
{
  var _url = Xrm.Page.getAttribute("new_linkedin").getValue();
  var _regex = /^http:\/\/www.linkedin.com\/profile\/view\?.*/;

  if(!_url.match(_regex))
  {
    alert("The URL entered is not a LinkedIn profile!");
  }
}
```

7. **Save** and **Publish** your resource.

8. Add the `ValidateLinkedIn()` function to the `OnChange` event of the newly created form field.

9. **Save** and **Publish** your solution.

10. Test your solution by navigating to the **Contact** form and entering a generic URL to any page. You should be prompted with the following message from the alert line.

11. Then enter a URL to a LinkedIn user profile. You should not be getting any more prompts.

How it works...

The script example provided reads the user input in the same way we read any regular text field, and then it compares it against a defined regular expression. For any non-mapping values, we prompt the users.

There's more...

While this is all nice, there are some limitations of the URL formatted text field.

This formatting is not supported in the header and footer of a form. As seen in the following screenshot, the **Other URL** field showing in the header of a **Contact** form is not formatted as a link, but rather as simple text:

See also

> ► For additional details on using the formatted **URL** field, see the documentation in the resource center `http://rc.crm.dynamics.com/rc/2011/en-us/on-prem/5.0/help/ug_cust_entity_fields.htm`.

Validating the ticker symbol field

The default ticker symbol field in Dynamics CRM 2011 is integrated with MSN Money to bring up information about the entered symbol. When this symbol is not found, the user is faced with an *Information Not Available* page. Unfortunately, only the website will validate the user input, not your CRM application. For us to validate the symbols, we need to implement an additional piece of functionality. We can thus prompt the user once they have entered the symbol if the input is not valid.

Getting ready

In order to work through the steps of creating a ticker symbol field, use an existing solution or create a new one.

How to do it...

Perform the following steps to customize a ticker symbol field on an **Account** form:

1. Add the **Account** entity to your solution, if not already added.

2. Open the main form to customize it.

3. Create a new field, name it `Ticker`, and set the **Type** to **Single Line of Text** and the **Format** to **Ticker Symbol**.

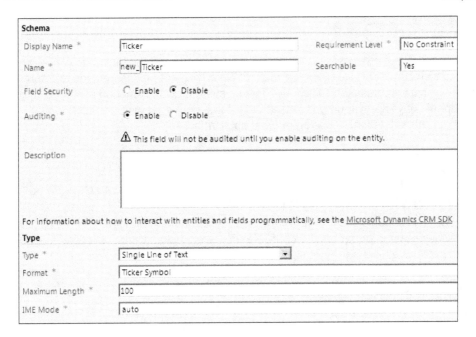

4. Add this new field to the form.

5. Test the form to make sure the new field appears and observe the default behavior. By default, the **Ticker Symbol** formatting adds a link to the text entered, and forwards the user to Microsoft Money on a click.

 Please note that out of the box there is no ticker symbol validation. Only when you click on the link, the resulting page will look up the symbol entered, and will bring back the **Search** page.

6. Add a new JScript web resource to your project, and add the following function to validate a ticker symbol. Add this function to the OnChange form field event.

```
function CheckTicker()
{
  var tickerValue = Xrm.Page.getAttribute("new_ticker").
getValue();
  if(!CheckTicker(tickerValue))
  {
    alert("The Ticker symbol provided does not exist!");
  }
}
```

7. **Save** and **Publish** your solution.

How it works...

The function we just presented does nothing more than to read the user input value, and pass it to a custom `CheckTicker()` function. We are expecting this function to return true if the value is a valid value, or false if not. Please customize this function according to the requirements of your environment. You can use some of the free web services available on the web for this validation, or use an internal application.

There's more...

Re-routing your request to another provider:

For an on-premise deployment, if you want to re-route your request to an internal application that provides ticker information, the configuration for the ticker symbol is located in an HTC file at the following location:

```
C:\Program Files\Microsoft Dynamics CRM\CRMWeb\_static\_form\
controls\INPUT.text.ticker.htc
```

You can override the JScript function in that file, and replace the line with `safeWindowOpen(Mscrm.CrmUri.create(...` to point to the URL of your custom application. This way, for an internal deployment where users are blocked from accessing the internet, the ticker link will forward them to your other internal application that provides stock information.

Please note that this customization is not supported, as it works using standard JavaScript and not the Dynamics CRM script API.

See also

▶   There are a few available APIs that will allow you to work with ticker symbols. Yahoo has a pretty good API for various financial web services. For additional details see `http://developer.yahoo.com/finance/company.html`.

Formatting phone numbers

Working with phone numbers and fax numbers is probably one of the most common tasks users will perform. As such, the system is flexible enough to allow you as a developer to customize these fields to your heart's content.

Getting ready

In order to follow through the steps of this example you need a solution created in your development environment.

How to do it...

The following steps will guide you through adding a JScript web resource that holds your phone number validation and formatting script, as well as associating it with one of the phone number fields on a form.

1. Open your solution, and create a new JScript resource.

2. Add the following function to your resource:

```
// call this function to format any north american phone number
(10 digit)
// in the following format: (xxx) xxx-xxxx
// pass context to the function
function FormatPhoneNo(context) {
    try {
        var nvsField = context.getEventSource().getValue();
        var nvsTmp = nvsField;

        if (typeof (nvsField) != "undefined" && nvsField != null)
{
            nvsTmp = nvsField.replace(/[^0-9]/g, "");
            switch (nvsTmp.length) {
                case 10:
                    nvsTmp = "(" + nvsTmp.substr(0, 3) + ") " +
nvsTmp.substr(3, 3) + "-" + nvsTmp.substr(6, 4);
                    break;

                default:
                    alert("Phone must contain 10 numeric
digits.");
                    break;
            }
        }
        context.getEventSource().setValue(nvsTmp);
    }
    catch (err) {
    }
}
```

3. Associate this function with the `OnChange` event of one of the phone fields on a **Contact** entity. Make sure that you pass the context to this function by selecting the context check-box.

How it works...

One thing you will observe us doing differently in this function is the fact that we are using the context rather than going straight to a specific field. What this allows us to do is reuse this same function for multiple phone and fax fields. We are retrieving the value of the field through the context, using the following expression:

```
var nvsField = context.getEventSource().getValue();
```

Next, we are checking that we have a valid value in the variable, cleaning all characters that are not numbers, and checking the length. As the comment states at the beginning of the function, we are using this format for standard North-American phone number formats, with a length of 10 digits.

You might want to work in conjunction with the **Country** field and format the phone numbers according to the country they belong to. This way you can handle formats for any country your system users will work with.

There's more...

Formatting phone numbers should be handled differently for regular browsers versus mobile devices. While on a browser, you have all the real estate of a large screen, on a mobile device you have to be mindful of the screen size and the lack of ability to tab between applications easily. For this reason, when developing mobile forms, we have to take into consideration all the available tricks in our bag to make a user's life as easy as possible.

Formatting for mobile forms

You will observe that in many instances you need to collect an extension for a telephone number. While this is easily done by adding an additional text field, when using mobile devices you might want to take a slightly different approach.

The mobile pages can be customized independently of the regular forms. This allows us to customize the telephone field, and add the extension properly, so a user with a smart phone can dial directly. Remember the old "pause" character? It is none other than the "," character. Knowing this, we can set the phone number on the mobile pages to include the extension, by formatting it such as `+XXX-XXX-XXXX,XXXX`.

Using such a format allows a user to tap on the phone number and dial directly. The users don't need to remember what extension he/she needs to dial. They will love you for making their life easier, and adoption will increase dramatically.

Formatting postal codes

Working with postal codes is again left to the latitude of developers. With the wide range of countries supported, it would be unrealistic to try to provide the functionality out of the box.

Getting ready

Using the previously created solution or a new solution, we will add postal code formatting for the **Account** entity.

How to do it...

Take the following steps to format a postal code:

1. Add a JScript web resource to hold your script.
2. Add the following script to the resource:

```
// Function to format postal code
 // for both Canadian and US postal codes
 function FormatPostalCode(context)
 {
  var oField = context.getEventSource().getValue();
  var sTmp;

  if(typeof(oField) != "undefined" && oField != null)
  {
  // check for US ZIP code
  if(oField.match(/^[0-9]{5}$/))
  {
    context.getEventSource().setValue(oField);
    return true;
  }

  // check for Canadian postal code
  sTmp = oField.toUpperCase();
  if (sTmp.match(/^[A-Z][0-9][A-Z][0-9][A-Z][0-9]$/))
  {
    sTmp = sTmp.substr(0,3) + " " + sTmp.substr(3,3);
    context.getEventSource().setValue(sTmp);
    return true;
  }
  if (sTmp.match(/^[A-Z][0-9][A-Z].[0-9][A-Z][0-9]$/))
```

```
    {
      context.getEventSource().setValue(sTmp);
      return true;
    }

    // code is invalid
    // alert("Incorrect ZIP/Postal Code format.");
    // code could be any other country, so leave as is
    }
    }
```

3. Add your function to the `OnChange` event of the postal code field you want to validate and format.

4. **Save** and **Publish** your customizations.

How it works...

As with our previous example, we are reading the value based on the context we are passing, so we can reuse this function across multiple postal code fields on various forms.

Using regular expressions, we are validating that the format of the user input is either five numeric characters or a combination of six alternating characters as required for the Canadian postal code. This piece can easily be changed to map to any other country's postal code format.

The section commented out at the end allows us to notify the user if the postal code entered does not correspond to any of the required formats. We can take additional actions here, by either clearing the field using `context.getEventSource().setValue("");` or just simply leaving the input as it is.

Alternatively you can use a web service to validate postal codes and addresses. Most international postal services will provide, for a price, a listing of all postal codes and associated addresses.

Replacing the Country and Province fields with lookups

Even though we touched on bits and pieces of this recipe earlier in the previous chapters, I will be presenting here a top-to-bottom approach of replacing the standard out-of-the-box **Country** and **Province** fields with lookups. This solution will allow users to select these values from pre-defined available options, and eliminate the issues resulting from typical user input errors.

Getting ready

For this recipe, use one of the solutions created in earlier chapters, or create a new one. Add to your solution the **Account** and **Contact** entities where we will replace the fields with lookups.

How to do it...

Follow the same steps on both the **Account** and the **Contact** entities. I will only describe the process once. You can follow the same process if you create a custom **Address** entity, or anywhere else where you need to capture address information.

The end result will be a transformation of the following field set:

To the following:

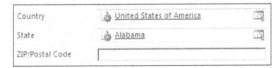

1. Open your existing solution.

2. Add a new entity named `Country`, with an internal name of `new_country`.

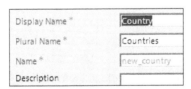

3. Make it visible only on the **Settings** area:

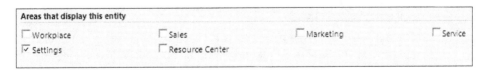

4. **Save** your new entity.

5. Open the main form of the entity, and modify the form as follows:

   1. Add a field named `Country Code`, with an internal name of `new_countrycode`. Format it as text, with a maximum length of 3. This field will hold an abbreviated version such as USA, CA, and UK.

   2. Add a field named `Display Sequence`, with an internal name of `new_displaysequence`. Format it as a whole number, with a minimum value of 0. I have set the maximum to 500, but you could set it to the total number of countries, which at the time of this writing stands at 196.

   3. Add these fields to your form for an end result as follows:

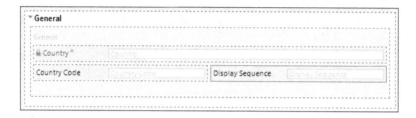

6. Add a new entity named `State`, with an internal name of `new_state`.

7. Make it visible only on the **Settings** area.

8. **Save** your new entity.

9. Open the main form of the entity, and customize it as follows:

   1. Add a new field named `State Code`, with an internal name of `new_statecode`. Format it as text, with a maximum length of 5, or enough to capture a short name for the state. Usually for US and Canada two characters are enough.

   2. Add a new field name `Display Sequence`, with an internal name of `new_displaysequence`. Format it as a whole number, with a minimum value of 0. Set the maximum depending on the number of provinces/states you intend to capture in the system. If unsure, set it to a value high enough for your initial phase. You can always change the maximum value at a later time.

3. Add a new field named `Country`, with an internal name of `new_country`. Format it as type lookup, with a target record type pointing back to the `Country` entity we have just created.

4. Add these new fields to your form, for an end result as follows:

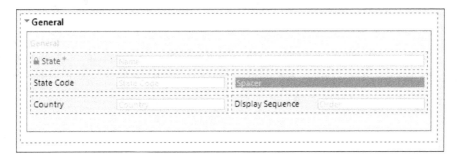

10. **Save** your new entity.

11. **Publish** all changes to this solution.

12. Open your **Account** entity or the entity where we will replace the standard text fields with our new lookups. Open the main form for editing.

13. Add a new field named State, with an internal name of new_state. Make the field type lookup, with a target record type of **State** (the entity we created earlier). Add this field to our form right underneath our existing **State/Province** field.

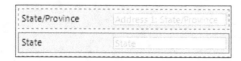

14. Similarly, add a new field named Country, with an internal name of new_country. Make the field type lookup, with a target record type of Country (the entity we created earlier). Add this field to our form.

15. Double-click the **State** field we just added, and on the **Display** tab, in the **Related Records Filtering** area, check the box next to **Only show records where:**.

16. Configure as in the following image:

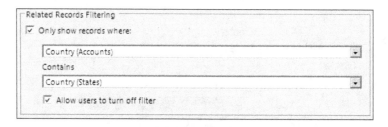

17. Turn off the check box on **Allow users to turn off filter**, so that users will always get a listing of the provinces related to the country selected.

18. In order to make the input work, move the country selection above the **State**. This allows the users to select a country first, and then get a listing of all state/provinces related to the country they already selected.

19. Make the default fields for **State/Province** and **Country/Region** not visible, by opening the field properties window, and unchecking the **Visible by default** checkbox.

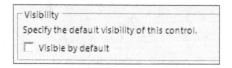

20. I have arranged the fields on the form as follows:

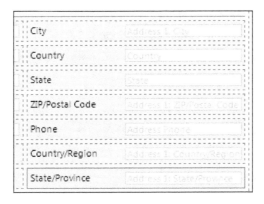

21. **Save** and **Publish** your entire solution.

22. Refresh your browser window to see the two new entities we have just created. Navigate to the **Settings** section. You should see them listed as follows in the **Extensions** area.

23. Open first the **Countries**, and add a few sample records.

24. Open next the **States** and add a few states/provinces for each of the added countries.

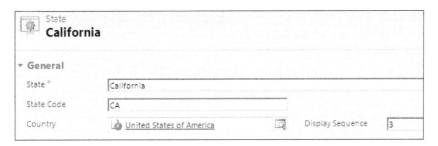

25. Once you have some sample data, check the **Account** form to make sure the filtering indeed takes place.

 The **Display Sequence** field can be used to order the views.

26. In order to keep the out-of-the-box functionality in place, and to allow some of the standard reports and views to function as expected, we will add two functions that will help us copy the values selected by the user in the lookup fields to the standard text fields that we have just marked as hidden.

27. Add a JScript web resource, and insert the following two functions:

```
function UpdateCountry()
{
  var _country = new Array();
  _country = Xrm.Page.getAttribute("new_country").getValue();
  if(_country != null)
  {
   Xrm.Page.getAttribute("address1_country").setValue(
    _country[0].name);
  }
}

function UpdateState()
{
  var _state = new Array();
  _state = Xrm.Page.getAttribute("new_state").getValue();
  if(_state != null)
  {
    Xrm.Page.getAttribute("address1_stateorprovince").setValue
    (_state[0].name);
  }
}
```

28. Associate the `UpdateCountry()` function with the `OnChange` event of the new country lookup we created, and the `UpdateState()` function to the `OnChange` event of the new `State` lookup.

29. Update a few records, and check using **Advanced Find** to make sure that the original fields are being also populated.

How it works...

The process I am following in this recipe is relatively simple. We are creating the related lookups, and populating the selected values into the original fields using the JavaScript functions. We could have done this without copying the values into the original fields, but the reason I chose to do so is because now I can use all the views and reports as defined out of the box, and any future upgrades or other solutions that are referencing those fields will find them also populated with the current values.

4

Rules and Events

In this chapter, we will cover the following topics:

- ▸ Form load event usage
- ▸ Form save event usage
- ▸ Field change event usage
- ▸ Working with tabs and sections
- ▸ Combining events
- ▸ Enforcing business rules

Introduction

Handling specific events is something everybody expects from an application. While JavaScript has its own event handling model, working with Dynamics CRM offers a different set of events that we can take advantage of.

 The JavaScript event model, while it might work, is not supported, and definitely not the approach you want to take when working within the context of Dynamics CRM.

Some of the most notable events and their counterparts in JavaScript are described in the following table:

Dynamics CRM 2011	JavaScript	Description
`OnLoad`	`onload`	This is a form event. Executes when a form is loaded. Most common use is to filter and hide elements on the form.
`OnSave`	`onsubmit`	This is a form event. It executes when a form is saved. Most common use is to stop an operation from executing, as a result of a failed validation procedure.
`TabStateChange`	n/a	This is a form event. It executes when the `DisplayState` of the tab changes.
`OnChange`	`onchange`	This is a field specific event. It executes when tabbing out of a field where you've changed the value. Please note that there is no equivalent for `onfocus` and `onblur`.
`OnReadyStateComplete`	n/a	This event indicates that the content of an IFrame has completed loading.

Additional details on Dynamics CRM 2011 specific events can be found on MSDN at

`http://msdn.microsoft.com/en-us/library/gg334481.aspx.`

Form load event usage

In this recipe, we will focus on executing a few operations triggered by the form load event. We can check the value of a specific field on the form, and based on that we can decide to hide a tab, hide a field, and prepopulate a text field with a predefined value.

Getting ready...

Just as with any of the previous recipes, you will need access to an environment, and permissions to make customizations. You should be a system administrator, a system customizer, or a custom role configured to allow you to perform the following operations.

How to do it...

For the purpose of this exercise, we will add to the **Contact** entity a new tab called "Special Customer", with some additional custom fields. We will also add an option set that we will check to determine if we hide or not the fields, as well as two new fields: one text field and one lookup field. So let's get started!

1. Open the contact's main form for editing.

2. Add a new tab by going to **Insert | Tab | One Column**.

3. Double-click on the newly added tab to open the **Tab Properties** window.

4. Change the **Label** field of the tab to Special Customer.

5. Make sure the show label is expanded by default and visible checkboxes are checked. Click on **OK**.

6. Add a few additional text fields on this tab. We will be hiding the tab along with the content within the tab.

7. Add a new field, named **Is Special Customer (new_IsSpecialCustomer)**. Leave the default yes/no values.

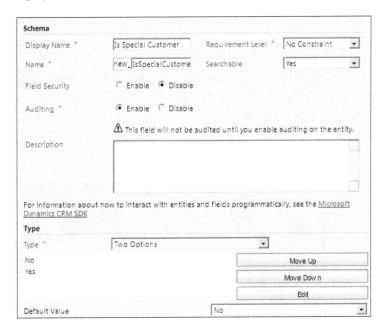

8. Add the newly created field to the general form for the contact.

9. Add another new text field, named **Customer Classification** (**new_CustomerClassification**). Leave the **Format** as **Text**, and the default **Maximum Length** to **100**, as shown in the following screenshot:

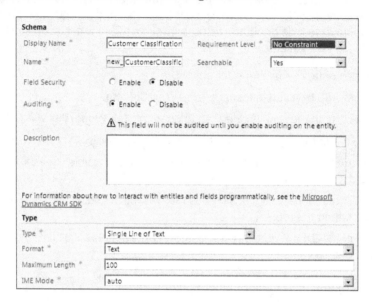

10. Add the newly created text field to the general form, under the previously added field.

11. Add a new lookup field, called **Partner** (**new_Partner**). Make it a lookup for a contact, as shown in the following screenshot:

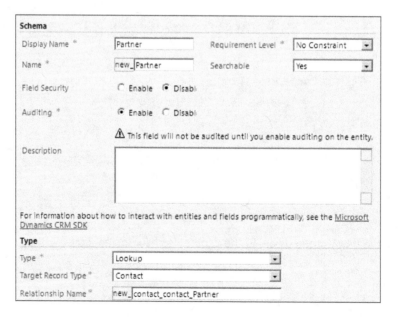

12. Add this new field to the general form, under the other two fields.

13. **Save** and **Publish** the **Contact** form.

14. Your form should look similar to the following screenshot:

 Observe the fact that I have ordered the three fields one on top of the other. The reason for this is because the default tab order in CRM is vertical and across. This way, when all the fields are visible, I can tab right from one to another.

15. In your solution where you made the previous changes, add a new web resource named **FormLoader** (**new_FormLoader**). Set the **Type** to **JScript**.

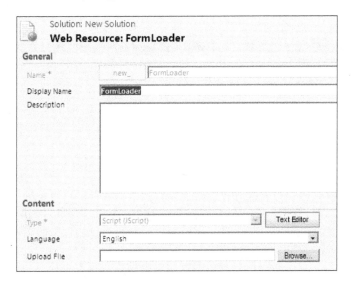

16. Click on the **Text Editor** button and insert the following function:

```
function IsSpecialCustomer()
{
  var _isSpecialSelection = null;
  var _isSpecial = Xrm.Page.getAttribute("new_isspecialcustomer");
  if(_isSpecial != null)
  {
    _isSpecialSelection = _isSpecial.getValue();
```

```
      }

      if(_isSpecialSelection == false)
      {
        // hide the Special Customer tab
        Xrm.Page.ui.tabs.get("tab_5").setVisible(false);
        // hide the Customer Classification field
        Xrm.Page.ui.controls.get("new_customerclassification").
        setVisible(false);
      // hide the Partner field
        Xrm.Page.ui.controls.get("new_partner").setVisible(false);
      }
    }
```

17. **Save** and **Publish** the web resource.

18. Go back to the **Contact** form, and on the ribbon select **Form Properties**.

19. On the **Events** tab, add the library created as web resource in the **Forms Libraries** section, and in the **Event Handlers** area, on the `Form OnLoad` add the function we created:

20. Click on **OK**, then click on **Save** and **Publish** the form.

21. Test your configuration by opening a new contact, setting the **Is Special Customer** field to **No**. Save and close the contact. Open it again, and the tab and fields should be hidden.

How it works...

The whole idea of this script is not much different from what we have demonstrated in some of the previous recipes. Based on a set form value, we hide a tab and some fields. Where we capture the difference is where we set the script to execute. Working with scripts executing when the form loads gives us a whole new way of handling various scenarios.

There's more...

In many scenarios, working with the form load events in conjunction with the other field events can potentially result in a very complex solution.

 When debugging, always pay close attention to the type of event you associate your script function with.

See also

See the *Combining events* recipe towards the end of this chapter for a more complex recipe detailing how to work with multiple events to achieve the expected result.

Form save event usage

While working with the `Form OnLoad` event can help us format and arrange the user interface, working with the `Form OnSave` opens up a new door towards validation of user input and execution of business process amongst others.

Getting ready

Using the same solution we have worked on in the previous recipe, we will continue to demonstrate a few other aspects of working with the forms in Dynamics CRM 2011. In this recipe the focus is on the handling the `Form OnSave` event.

How to do it...

First off, in order to kick off this, we might want to verify a set of fields for a condition, or perform a calculation based on a formula. In order to simplify this process, we can just check a simple yes/no condition on a form.

How it works...

Using the previously customized solution, we will be taking advantage of the **Contact** entity and the fields that we have already customized on that form. If you are starting with this recipe fresh, take the following step before delving into this recipe:

1. Add a new two-options field, named **Is Special Customer** (**new_IsSpecialCustomer**). Leave the default yes/no values.

Using this field, if the answer is **No**, we will stop the save process.

2. In your solution add a new web resource. I have named it `new_ch4rcp2`. Set its type to **JScript**.

3. Enter the following function in your resource:

```
function StopSave(context)
{
    var _isSpecialSelection = null;
```

```
    var _isSpecial = Xrm.Page.getAttribute("new_isspecialcustomer");

    if(_isSpecial != null)
    {
      _isSpecialSelection = _isSpecial.getValue();
    }

    if(_isSpecialSelection == false)
    {
      alert("You cannot save your record while the Customer is not a
      friend!");
      context.getEventArgs().preventDefault();
    }
}
```

4. The function basically checks for the value in our **Is Special Customer**. If a value is retrieved, and that value is `No`, we can bring up an alert and stop the `Save and Close` event.

5. Now, back on to the contact's main form, we attach this new function to the form's `OnSave` event.

6. **Save** and **Publish** your solution.

7. In order to test this functionality, we will create a new contact, populate all the required fields, and set the **Is Special Customer** field to **No**.

8. Now try to click on **Save and Close**.

9. You will get an alert as seen in the following screenshot, and the form will not close nor be saved.

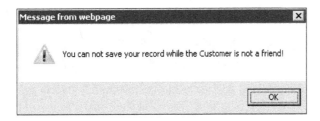

10. Changing the **Is Special Customer** selection to **Yes** and saving the form will now save and close the form.

There's more...

While this recipe only describes in a very simplistic manner the way to stop a form from saving and closing, the possibilities here are immense. Think about what you can do on form save, and what you can achieve if a condition should be met in order to allow the form to be saved.

Starting a process instead of saving the form

Another good use for blocking the save and close form is to take a different path. Let's say we want to kick off a workflow when we block the save form. We can call from the previous function a new function as follows:

```
function launchWorkflow(dialogID, typeName, recordId)
{
var serverUri = Mscrm.CrmUri.create('/cs/dialog/rundialog.aspx');
 window.showModalDialog(serverUri + '?DialogId=' + dialogID +
'&EntityName=' + typeName +
'&ObjectId=' + recordId, null, 'width=615,height=480,resizable=1,statu
s=1,scrollbars=1');
// Reload form
window.location.reload(true);
}
```

We pass to this function the following three parameters:

- GUID of the Workflow or Dialog
- The type name of the entity
- The ID of the record

See also

- For more details on parameters see the following article on MSDN:

  http://msdn.microsoft.com/en-us/library/gg309332.aspx

Field change event usage

In this recipe we will drill down to a lower level. We have handled form events, and now it is time to handle field events. The following recipe will show you how to bring all these together and achieve exactly the result you need.

Getting ready

For the purpose of this recipe, let's focus on reusing the previous solution. We will check the value of a field, and act upon it.

How to do it...

In order to walkthrough this recipe, follow these steps:

1. Create a new form field called **new_changeevent**, with a label of **Change Event**, and a **Type** of **Two Options**. Leave the default values of **No** and **Yes**. Leave the **Default Value** as **No**.

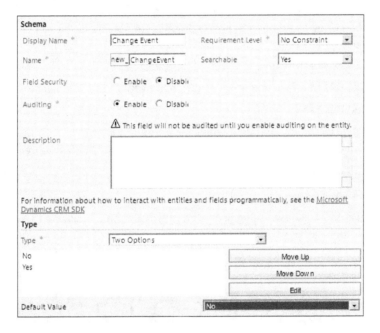

2. Add this field to your main **Contact** form.
3. Add the following script to a new JScript web resource:

```
function ChangeEvent()
{
  var _changeEventSelection = null;
  var _isChanged = Xrm.Page.getAttribute("new_changeevent");

  if(_isChanged != null)
  {
    _changeEventSelection = _isChanged.getValue();
```

```
        }

        if(_changeEventSelection == true)
        {
          alert("Change event is set to True");
          // perform other actions here
        }
        else
        {
          alert("Change event is set to False");
        }
    }
```

4. This function, as seen in the previous recipes, checks the value of the **Two Options** field, and performs and action based on the user selection. The action in this example is simply bringing an alert message up.

5. Add the new web resource to the form libraries.

6. Associate this new function to the OnChange event of the field we have just created.

7. **Save** and **Publish** your solution.

8. Create a new contact, and try changing the **Change Event** value from **No** to **Yes** and back. Every time the selection is changed, a different message comes up in the alert.

How it works...

Handling events at the field level, specifically the `OnSave` event, allows us to dynamically execute various other functions. We can easily take advantage of this functionality to modify the form displayed to a user dynamically, based on a selection. Based on a field value, we can define areas or field on the form to be hidden and shown.

Working with tabs and sections

This recipe will show you how to work with tabs and sections on a form. You might have observed some bits of code in other recipes that allow you to hide a specific tab if a condition is not met. Here, we will analyze how to hide and show these form elements.

Getting ready

For the purpose of this demonstration, we will be looking at the **Contact** form we have been working on until now. Reuse the same solution you have used already, or if you want to start a new one, create a new solution.

How to do it...

First off, let's focus on working with the tabs. These form elements have the advantage of generating a link on the navigation, allowing a user to browse directly to a specific tab. They come in handy when you have a long entity form, and you don't want the user to scroll for too long.

On the top-left side of the **Contact** form, right underneath the ribbon, your will see the tab as shown in the following screenshot:

Observe the four tabs displayed by default on the contact.

 Note that hiding a tab will not only hide the tab on the form, but will also remove the link in the tabs area.

We can show and hide tabs based on either a form event, such as the `OnLoad` or `OnSave` events, or based on a field event, such as the `OnChange` event. The code is the same, the only difference is what event we associate with our function.

For the purpose of this example, I want to hide a tab when the form loads, no matter what.

1. Add a new web resource of type **JScript**, and insert the following function:

```
function HideTab()
{
   Xrm.Page.ui.tabs.get("notes and activities").setVisible(false);
}
```

2. Add the new web resource to the form libraries.

3. Associate your function with the form `OnLoad` event.

4. **Save** and **Publish** your solution.

5. Test by creating a new contact. The **Notes & Activities** tab will be hidden.

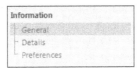

6. Also, the form section is hidden from the user.

In order to revert this action, check for a form condition and run another function to display this tab again. You can define the condition to be either a value populated in a text field, or maybe a new "Notes Required" two-options field on the form. Check the value as described in the previous recipes, and call the following function to show the tab:

```
function ShowTab()
{
   Xrm.Page.ui.tabs.get("notes and activities").setVisible(true);
}
```

Similarly with tabs, a form section is an area of the form situated within a tab. You can choose to leave the tab visible at all times, but hide or show only a section.

The following function hides a section on the **Contact** form on form load. For this case, I will be leaving the **Notes & Activities** tab visible, but I want to hide only the **Activities** section.

```
function HideSection()
{
   Xrm.Page.ui.tabs.get("notes and activities").sections.
get("activities").setVisible(false);
}
```

Observe that, in order to get to a section, we have to retrieve the tab on which the section lives.

On the flip side, in order to show a section back on the form, the following function does the job:

```
function ShowSection()
{
   Xrm.Page.ui.tabs.get("notes and activities").sections.
get("activities").setVisible(true);
}
```

 Note that these functions assume that the tabs and/or section are already created on the form, and are only dealing with hiding and/or showing these form elements.

How it works...

The demonstration in this recipe revolves around the concept of defining what the user needs to see on an entity form, based on either a form event or a predefined rule. We do count on all these tabs and sections being generated ahead of time. All we are doing is showing and/or hiding them according to our business rules.

Getting to a tab in order to perform an action on it is achieved using the following line of code:

```
Xrm.Page.ui.tabs.get("tabName")
```

Once we have a reference to the tab, we can perform the required actions on it, such as show or hide the tab by setting the `SetVisible` property.

Additionally, getting to a section on the form is done through the tab it lives on. The following code gets a reference to the section:

```
Xrm.Page.ui.tabs.get("tabName").sections.get("sectionName")
```

From here on, we can perform other actions.

Combining events

In the previous recipes of this chapter we have seen some examples on working with the form UI based on either a predefined rule on form load, or on a field's `onchange` event. This example will focus on putting it all together in order to achieve a comprehensive result that actually can satisfy a realistic business rule.

Getting ready

Let's go back to the solution that we have worked with in the previous recipe. We will be using the same **Contact** form to implement this example. Following the *Form load event usage* recipe described earlier in this chapter, we can easily realize that it only works first time when the user loads a contact. How about if the user changes a value on the form? We have touched on the functionality a little bit in the following recipes, but let's put it all together now.

How to do it...

The following is what we want to achieve:

- When a user opens a contact, if the contact is marked as special customer, we want to collect additional information about him/her.
- When a user opens a contact that is not marked as special customer, we want to hide the additional fields.
- When a user changes a contact from special to not special or back, we want the form to dynamically show or hide the fields.

Up until now, the first two conditions are met by the recipe described earlier. Now let's focus on the third requirements.

1. Open your existing solution from the first recipe in this chapter.
2. Open your JScript web resource in which you added the other functions.

3. Add the following new function to this resource:

```
function ChangeCustomer()
{
  var _isSpecialSelection = null;
  var _isSpecial = Xrm.Page.getAttribute("new_isspecialcustomer");

  if(_isSpecial != null)
  {
    _isSpecialSelection = _isSpecial.getValue();
  }

  if(_isSpecialSelection == false)
  {
    // hide the Special Customer tab
    Xrm.Page.ui.tabs.get("tab_5").setVisible(false);
    // hide the Customer Classification field
    Xrm.Page.ui.controls.get("new_customerclassification").
setVisible(false);
    // hide the Partner field
    Xrm.Page.ui.controls.get("new_partner").setVisible(false);
  }
  else if(_isSpecialSelection == true)
  {
    // show the Special Customer tab
    Xrm.Page.ui.tabs.get("tab_5").setVisible(true);
    // show the Customer Classification field
    Xrm.Page.ui.controls.get("new_customerclassification").
setVisible(true);
    // show the Partner field
    Xrm.Page.ui.controls.get("new_partner").setVisible(true);
  }
}
```

4. Associate this function with the **OnChange** event of the **Is Special Customer** field, as shown in the following screenshot:

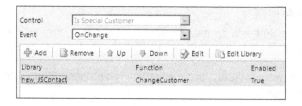

5. **Save** and **Publish** your solution.

6. Test your script by opening a contact, and changing the **Is Special Customer** value from **Yes** to **No** and back. You will observe the **Special Customer** tab being shown and hidden as you change the value, as well as the other two fields.

How it works...

Taking a closer look at the function presented earlier, there are really a handful of actions we take.

1. First off, we begin by declaring our temporary variable that will store the value of the **Is Special Customer** field. This being a two-options field, we expect back a `True`/ `False` value. We set this to `null`, note that if it does not get assigned we can skip execution of any other code:

   ```
   var _isSpecialSelection = null;
   ```

2. On the next line, we get a reference to the form field:

   ```
   var _isSpecial = Xrm.Page.getAttribute("new_isspecialcustomer");
   ```

3. In the next section, we check to make sure that our form field reference indeed found a field on the form, and we get the value of that field into the first variable we declared:

   ```
   if(_isSpecial != null)
   {
       _isSpecialSelection = _isSpecial.getValue();
   }
   ```

4. Based on the value retrieved from the form field, we can start to act on other form elements. Observe that first we check if the value is `false`, and then we hide the **Form** tab and fields:

   ```
   if(_isSpecialSelection == false)
   {
       // hide the Special Customer tab
       Xrm.Page.ui.tabs.get("tab_5").setVisible(false);
       // hide the Customer Classification field
       Xrm.Page.ui.controls.get("new_customerclassification").
   setVisible(false);
       // hide the Partner field
       Xrm.Page.ui.controls.get("new_partner").setVisible(false);
   }
   ```

5. Then we check if the value is `true` so we can show these elements back to the user:

   ```
   else if(_isSpecialSelection == true)
   {
       // show the Special Customer tab
   ```

```
Xrm.Page.ui.tabs.get("tab_5").setVisible(true);
// show the Customer Classification field
Xrm.Page.ui.controls.get("new_customerclassification").
setVisible(true);
// show the Partner field
Xrm.Page.ui.controls.get("new_partner").setVisible(true);
}
```

If the value is not assigned, and it remains null as we defined it at the beginning, we do not execute any code. If there is a requirement to execute an action for that case, you can easily add another `else if` block at the end.

There's more...

A few things we have to be aware of when designing our forms include the following aspects:

You cannot add new fields dynamically

Working with form elements in Dynamics CRM assumes that all these fields are precreated and added to the forms. You cannot dynamically create new form fields and add them.

Be mindful of form layout

While this might not catch your attention right away, depending on where you drop your field on the form, after a while you will observe that when you hide a field, the remaining fields underneath do not rearrange automatically. This is because, while you have your field hidden, it still exists on the page at that specified location.

When designing your page, arrange your individual fields that you will hide in such a way so that when you hide one, it does not leave an obvious gap on the form. Either place them at the bottom of a section or tab, or place them in such an order that while you start showing them, they get added at the bottom of the previous one. This works in a case where you have a business progression expected, and you display items on the form as you progress through phases predefined.

See also

> ▸ For additional references on using form programming, see the following MSDN article: http://msdn.microsoft.com/en-us/library/gg328261.aspx

Enforcing business rules

For this recipe, we will focus on a different entity. Let's have a look at Opportunity. The **Opportunity** is the result of a qualified lead in many cases, but Dynamics CRM allows you to also add opportunities directly.

With opportunities, one of the fields we will focus on is the pipeline phase. For specific scenarios, a pipeline phase is tracked, customized, and enforced. Business rules can define the stages that define each pipeline phase, and specific rules that have to be met for an opportunity to progress to the next pipeline phase.

Getting ready

We can start by either reusing one of the previously created solutions or creating a new one. If you do not have a solution created, start by creating one.

How to do it...

We assume the following business rules

- An Opportunity begins at 10 percent
- An Opportunity progresses to 25 percent if the **Rating** field is set to **Hot**
- An Opportunity progresses to 50 percent if a currency and price list are defined
- An Opportunity progresses to 75 percent if a freight amount is defined

We will achieve this by using a combination of scripting and workflows. So let's get to it.

1. Open your solution and add the **Opportunity** entity if not already added.
2. Go to processes and add a new process. Configure it as described in the following screenshot:

3. Once you click on **OK**, the process information window opens up. Set the following items on this window:
    1. Set the **Scope** to **Organization**
    2. Set the **Start when** to **Record is created**
    3. Add an **Update Record** step
    4. In the **Update** make sure **Opportunity** is selected
    5. Click on **Set Properties**

4. In the new form that opens find the **Pipeline Phase** field, and type in **10%**, as shown in the following screenshot:

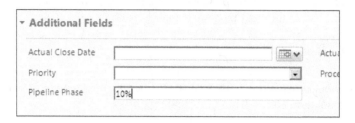

5. Click on **Save and Close**.

6. Your form now should look similar to the following screenshot:

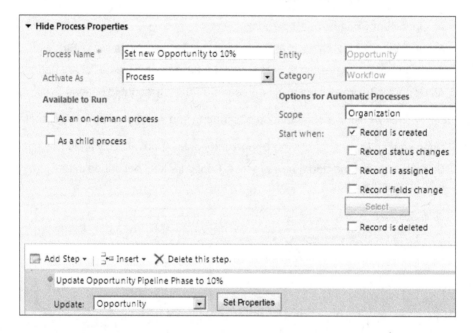

7. Click on **Save** and then **Activate** to activate your process.

8. Click on **Close**.

9. Now your processes window will show you the newly added process along with other processes previously added. Make sure that the **Status** shows **Activated**.

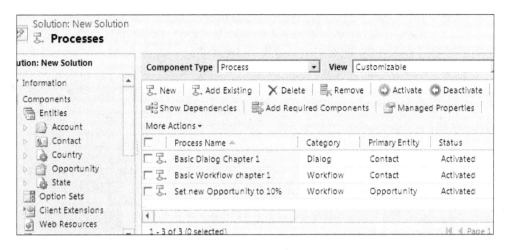

10. Once we have this process, let's open a new **Opportunity**, fill in the required fields, and click on **Save and Close**. Give it a moment for the workflow to execute.

11. Reopening the opportunity you just created should show you the customized **10%** value added in the footer of the page, as seen in the following screenshot:

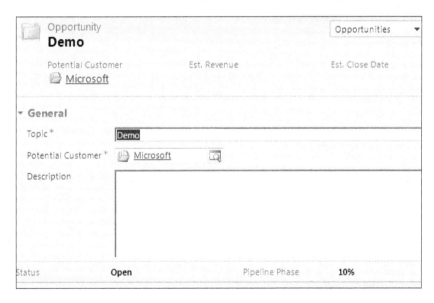

12. Add a new workflow that updates the pipeline phase to 25 percent. Configure it to kick off when the rating field changes value. We check if the rating value is **Hot**, and then we update the pipeline phase to 25 percent.

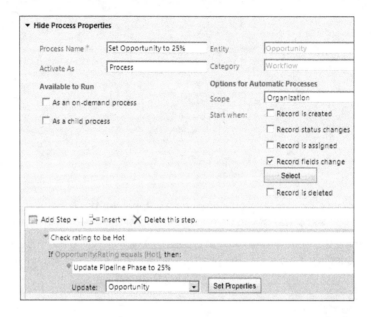

13. Now we have to check if the `Currency` and `Price List` are defined. We will perform this check in JScript, and update a temporary field with a `true`/`false` value. Add a two-options field to the form, named `new_progressto50`.

14. Insert the following script in a JScript resource, and associate it to the `OnChange` event of both the **Currency** (`transactioncurrencyid`) and **Price List** (`pricelevelid`) fields:

```
function HasCurrencyAndPriceList()
{
  var _currency = false;
  var _priceList = false;

  var currency = new Array();
  currency = Xrm.Page.getAttribute("transactioncurrencyid").
getValue();
  if(currency != null)
  {
    _currency = true;
  }

  var priceList = new Array();
  priceList = Xrm.Page.getAttribute("").getValue();
```

```
if(priceList != null)
{
  _priceList = true;
}

if(_currency == true && _priceList == true)
{
  // set temp field to true
  Xrm.Page.getAttribute("new_progressto50").setValue(true);
}
}
```

15. Create a new workflow similar to the previous one, that starts when the **Progress to 50%** field is changed, checks the field value, and if set to `True`, updates the pipeline phase to **50%**.

16. Finally, add a new workflow that starts when the **Freight Amount** field is changed, checks if the pipeline phase is at **50%** and if the amount contains a value greater or equal to **0.00**, and updates the pipeline phase to **75%**.

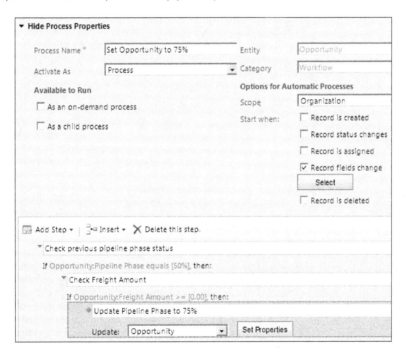

17. **Save** and **Publish** your solution.

18. Test your solution by filling in progressively the required fields and follow how the pipeline phase updates automatically.

How it works...

The solution presented here enforces business rules through the use of workflows, and shows an example where working with JScript in conjunction with workflows can achieve the expected result.

For the sake of simplicity, I have demonstrated the creation of four different workflows, one for each phase progression. In real life, you would build all these rules in a single workflow. Additionally, you would probably build a reversed process that would downgrade the pipeline phase if a system value is changed to a value that does not allow the opportunity to pass a lower threshold.

5
Error Handling

In this chapter we will cover:

- ▶ Handling unexpected user input
- ▶ Handling unexpected processing
- ▶ Blocking events
- ▶ Handling UI events
- ▶ Advanced error handling
- ▶ Adding a new account and contact with validation

Introduction

After focusing on working with standard elements of Dynamics CRM previously, we now turn our attention to unexpected situations in your scripts including a focus on input validation techniques, handling unexpected results, blocking events from taking place, and complex error handling.

 All scripting should include error handling. Previous examples did not include error handling to allow for clarity. However, in production, your code should always handle unexpected situations.

Handling unexpected user input

In this recipe we will be looking at how to handle unexpected user input. While this is already in place for some specific field types, we can easily enhance the system functionality through very simple validation scripts and user feedback messages.

Getting ready

Using one of the previously created solutions or creating a new solution, add the **Contact** entity to the solution. We will focus our attention on the **Contact** fields, but the same code can be applied to any standard or custom entities created in Dynamics CRM.

Some standard field formats in CRM include elements of user input validation. Upon data entry, users are prompted if their input is invalid, and the focus returns to the field, while the incorrect input is cleared. Take the date field as an example. Enter in a date field a string of `abc123` to observe the behavior. The following prompt gets displayed:

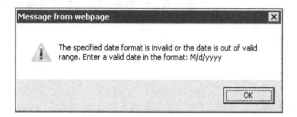

Once you click on **OK**, your input is cleared, and the focus is returned to the field you were trying to modify. But let's see how we can achieve the same result on a standard text field. We want to check that the input starts with a capital letter, is longer than three characters, and does not contain spaces. If these requirements are not met, we'll bring up a notification message, clear the field, and return the focus to it.

How to do it...

In order to test our script, we'll create a new text field. Perform the following steps to do so:

1. Create a new field named **Single Name** (`new_SingleName`). Set it to type single line of text, format of text, and a maximum length of 100.

2. Add your new field to the form.

3. Generate a new JScript resource in your solution, named `new_JSUserInput`.

4. Add the following function to your resource:

```
function CheckUserInput()
{
    var _userInput = Xrm.Page.getAttribute("new_singlename").
getValue();
    var _isValid = false;
    if(_userInput != null && _userInput != "")
    {
        if(_userInput.match(/^[A-Z][a-z]+$/))
        {
```

```
      _isValid = true;
    }
  }

  if(_isValid == false)
  {
    // clear the field
    _userInput = "";
    Xrm.Page.getAttribute("new_singlename").
    setValue(_userInput);
    // alert
    alert("The input is not valid!");
    // set focus
    Xrm.Page.getControl("firstname").setFocus(true);
    Xrm.Page.getControl("new_singlename").setFocus(true);
  }
}
```

5. Associate this function to the `OnChange` event of the **Single Name** field we created.

6. Save and publish.

There are two parts of this function, as follows:

▸ In the first part, we retrieve the user input, we check to make sure that there is in fact some input, and we run it against a regular expression.

▸ In the second part, once we have determined that there is no match, we execute our script to clear the field, bring up the notification alert for the user, and set the focus back to the same field.

> You have probably observed that I have set the focus twice, first to the First Name field, and second time back to our field. The first time when you set the focus, you can use any field on the form. The reason for doing that is, if you set the focus directly on your custom field, it will not work. Back in Dynamics CRM Version 4 a hotfix was released to address this issue. You can find out more information at the following URL:
>
> `http://support.microsoft.com/?scid=kb;en-us;953291&x=10&y=4`

There's more...

Using regular expressions is a very handy way of validating user input. I suggest you pay close attention to the regular expression syntax. For additional details, a good starting point is w3schools at `http://www.w3schools.com/jsref/jsref_obj_regexp.asp`.

See also

The following URLs can be referred to for further information:

▶ Hotfix for the `SetFocus` functionality in Dynamics CRM 4.0 available at `http://support.microsoft.com/?scid=kb;en-us;953291&x=10&y=4`

▶ Additional regular expressions details at `http://www.w3schools.com/jsref/jsref_obj_regexp.asp`

Handling unexpected processing

While this recipe will most likely not introduce you to anything specific to Dynamics CRM, the error-handling procedures described here are specific to the JavaScript language and can easily be applied in the context of Dynamics CRM. Full support of the JavaScript try/catch exception-handler block was introduced around the release of Internet Explorer Version 6.

JavaScript defines six standard and one custom error type to allow you to throw your own customized exceptions. They are given in the following table:

Error	Details
URIError	This error occurs while encoding or decoding an URI. It is not a common occurrence in Dynamics CRM.
RangeError	This error occurs when the number is out of range. It has a quite common occurrence when performing calculations, especially when overriding the standard taxation in Dynamics CRM.
ReferenceError	This error is caused by an illegal reference; this is returned in Internet Explorer as a `TypeError`.
EvalError	This error can be generated while using the `eval()` function. This is also returned in Internet Explorer as a `TypeError`.
TypeError	This error is not as common anymore when defining most of your variables as `var`, but you will encounter this in the case of incorrect casting.
SyntaxError	Working in conjunction with `EvalError`, this error is thrown when there is a syntax error within the `eval()` function. This does not catch the standard syntax errors.

In addition to these error types, catching default syntax errors can be done by using the standard `onerror` event of the window. The syntax for that is as follows:

```
window.onerror = function(parameters){
  // processing
}
```

Add this to the script section of the head.

Getting ready

Either open any one of the previously created solutions, or create a new one. We will be focusing again on the **Contact** entity.

How to do it...

To handle unexpected processing, perform the following steps:

1. Open the **Contact** entity's main form for editing.

2. Add a new option set named **Errors** (new_errors), with options such as `URIError`, `RangeError`, `ReferenceError`, `EvalError`, `TypeError`, `SyntaxError`, and `CustomError`.

3. Add the field to your form.

4. Save and publish the form.

5. Create a new JScript web resource in your solution. Name it **JS Errors** (new_jserrors).

6. Add the following function to your resource:

```
function ErrorHandler()
{
  var _error = Xrm.Page.getAttribute("new_errors").
  getSelectedOption().text;
  // alert("Selected option is: " + _error);

  switch(_error)
  {
    case "URIError":
      try
      {
        decodeURIComponent("%");
      }
      catch(err)
      {
```

```
      alert(err.name + " || " + err.message);
    }
    break;
  case "RangeError":
    var _age = 120;
    try
    {
      if(_age > 100)
      {
        throw new RangeError("Age cannot be over 100");
      }
    }
    catch(err)
    {
      alert(err.name + " || " + err.message);
    }
    break;
  case "ReferenceError":
    try
    {
      // use an undeclared variable
      trying.thisone;
      // TypeError due to browser
    }
    catch(err)
    {
      alert(err.name + " || " + err.message);
    }
    break;
  case "EvalError":
    // not used in recent versions, but supported
    try
    {
      var y = new eval();
      // TypeError due to browser
    }
    catch(err)
    {
      alert(err.name + " || " + err.message);
    }
    break;
  case "TypeError":
    try
```

```
    {
      var _obj = {};
      // call undefined method
      _obj.execute();
    }
    catch(err)
    {
      alert(err.name + " || " + err.message);
    }
    break;
  case "SyntaxError":
    try
    {
      var _x = "some string";
      var _y = 10;
      var _total = eval(_x + _y);
    }
    catch(err)
    {
      alert(err.name + " || " + err.message);
    }
    break;
  case "CustomError":
    try
    {
      throw new Error("Custom Error message");
    }
    catch(err)
    {
      alert(err.name + " || " + err.message);
    }
    break;
  default:
    // do nothing
  }
}
```

7. Associate the `ErrorHandler` function to the `OnChange` event of the field we created.

8. Save and publish your solution.

9. Test the function by changing the values in the option set.

How it works...

Selecting each of the option set values will generate the specific error. The following events take place:

1. **Generating a URIError**: We are decoding a string that is not a valid URL, resulting in the following type of error:

    ```
    try
      {
         decodeURIComponent("%");
      }
    ```

2. **Generating a RangeError**: In this example we are checking that a defined age is lower than 100, and we throw a new `RangeError` with our own custom message:

    ```
    var _age = 120;
    try
      {
         if(_age > 100)
         {
            throw new RangeError("Age cannot be over 100");
         }
      }
    ```

3. **Generating a ReferenceError**: A reference error is the result of, in this case, trying to access a variable or method that is not defined. Observe though that when running this code, you will see a `TypeError` instead. That is the default browser behavior, as follows:

    ```
    try
    {
      // use an undeclared variable
      trying.thisone;
      // TypeError due to browser
    }
    ```

4. **Generating an EvalError**: An `EvalError`, while not a common one, is the result of using the `eval` function in an unsupported manner. In this case, we use it as a declaration. Again, due to browser-specific interpretation, the actual error returned is a `TypeError`:

    ```
    try
    {
      var y = new eval();
      // TypeError due to browser
    }
    ```

5. **Generating a TypeError**: Aside from the previously mentioned cases, a `TypeError` is the result of a call to an undefined function as per our example:

```
try
{
  var _obj = {};
  // call undefined method
  _obj.execute();
}
```

6. **Generating a SyntaxError**: Contrary to the name of this error, it does not have anything to do with improper syntax. When encountering improper syntax, the error you will see will be more along the lines of the following screenshot:

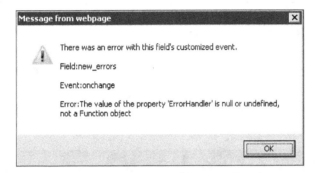

A `SyntaxError` is the result of improper use of the `eval()` function. In our example we are evaluating the sum of a string with an integer, thus resulting in a syntax error:

```
try
{
  var _x = "some string";
  var _y = 10;
  var _total = eval(_x + _y);
}
```

7. **Generating a custom error**: Aside from throwing any of the standard errors, we can throw a generic error as described in our example. In such a situation we can define our custom error message:

```
try
{
  throw new Error("Custom Error message");
}
```

There's more...

As mentioned before, there are certain standard JavaScript errors that are returned by IE as a different error type. These are `EvalError` and the `ReferenceError`. They both are returned in IE 8 and 9 as a `TypeError`. This is not a script problem, but rather it is a browser-specific interpretation.

Throwing custom errors

In certain situations you will want to throw your own custom errors in the code. You can use this approach to satisfy various failure points at different stages in the code. In order to determine which error was thrown, check the message or include a custom error ID in your message.

See also

▶ Error object reference at `http://msdn.microsoft.com/en-us/library/dww52sbt(v=vs.94)`

▶ JavaScript Syntax errors at `http://msdn.microsoft.com/en-us/library/6bby3x2e(v=vs.94).aspx`

Blocking events

One of the most common requirements that you will eventually encounter is to block a form from getting saved if a certain condition is not met.

Getting ready

Use any of the previously created solutions, or if starting at this recipe create a new solution for this exercise. Add the **Contact** entity to your solution.

How to do it...

To block events, perform the following steps:

1. Within your solution, navigate to **Entities | Contact | Forms** and open the **Contact** main form for editing. Add a new field of type **Two Options**. Name it Can Save (new_cansave) and leave the default **Yes** and **No** values.

2. Add the field to your form.

3. Save and publish the form.

4. Add a new web resource named **JS Event Blocking** (new_JSEventBlocking).

5. Insert the following code:

```
function BlockSave(context)
{
  var _canSave = Xrm.Page.getAttribute("new_cansave").
  getSelectedOption().text;
  if(_canSave == "No")
  {
    Xrm.Page.context.getEventArgs().preventDefault();
  }
}
```

6. Save and publish the resource.

7. Associate the BlockSave function to the form `OnSave` event. Make sure you check the checkbox for **Pass execution context as first parameter**.

8. Save and publish your solution.

9. Open a contact or create a new one. Set the **Can Save** field to **No**, and click on **Save** or **Save and Close**. Your form will not get saved anymore.

10. Return the **Can Save** to **Yes**, and click on **Save** or **Save and Close**. Now your form gets saved as expected.

 It's usually a good idea to notify the user that you've blocked the form save, and provide a reason why. Also, for usability, consider setting the focus back on the field where the input value is not within the expected parameters.

How it works...

In this example the rule is as simplistic as it can get. We read the value of **Can Save**, and if the value is **No**, then we block the form from getting saved. In a real-life situation your condition will definitely be more complex than that. It could be driven by a set of fields, a complex calculation, or any other business rule. For simplicity, you can always create a hidden field similar to our **Can Save** field, and based on the business rules set the value accordingly. Then your script to prevent a save is kept clear of your main logic.

There's more...

The opposite of stopping a form from getting saved has a few variations. We can look at either the simple straightforward **Save**, **Save and New**, or **Save and Close**.

Forcing a Save

In order to force a save in JavaScript, incorporate the following line of code in a function that you can call when needed:

```
Xrm.Page.data.entity.save();
```

Save and New

To execute the same functionality from the **Save and New** button, incorporate the following line in your function:

```
Xrm.Page.data.entity.save('saveandnew');
```

Save and Close

Just like Save and New, we can call the same line of code, and pass a different parameter in order to achieve the **Save and Close** functionality:

```
Xrm.Page.data.entity.save('saveandclose');
```

See also

In Update Rollup 8 for Dynamics CRM 2011, an issue was fixed that was preventing using scripting to cancel the OnSave event in a recurring appointment. This is documented with the release notes. Additional details are found on the Update Rollup 8 page at http://support.microsoft.com/kb/2600644.

Handling UI events

For the instances where you need to block the form from getting saved due to a user input error I have mentioned briefly, it's always a good idea to return a message to the user and notify them of the reason for such a decision. The option specified results in returning an alert message to the user.

In other situations, you will find that posting a message on the form itself can be much more efficient. For one, it does not require an additional click of the mouse. Also, you can create a tally of all the messages, and display them all in one single spot, formatted to stand out.

 This recipe describes a customization approach that is not officially supported. The reason for this is that referencing the form elements is done outside of the standard Dynamics CRM object model. We are using the HTML/JavaScript page object model. Even though it's not officially supported, this type of customization has been available and functional since version 4.0.

Getting ready

For the purpose of this recipe, we will be either reusing any one of the previous solutions or creating a new one. We will be making our changes on the **Contact** form. For simplicity, we will only validate a single field, and return an error message on the form. You can later expand that functionality to incorporate validation of multiple fields, and return all the custom error messages in the same dialogue box on the form.

How to do it...

To handle UI events perform the following steps:

1. Open the **Contact** main form for editing.
2. Create a new custom field named **Message** (new_message) of the type **Two Options**.
3. Add it to the form.
4. Create a new single line of text field named **Placeholder** (new_placeholder).
5. Place it on the form all the way at the top of the **Name** section of the **General** tab. Set its **Formatting** to **Two Columns**.
6. Modify the field's properties. Uncheck the **Display label on the form** checkbox, as shown in the following screenshot:

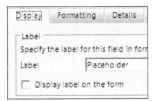

7. Save and publish the form.
8. Add a new JScript web resource, named **JS Message Box** (new_JSMessageBox).
9. Add a function that will launch on the form's load, named contactLoad. This function will hide the **Placeholder** field we have created. The purpose of the **Placeholder** field is to define the location where our custom message will be displayed on the form:

```
function contactLoad()
{
  var _placeholder = document.
  getElementById("new_placeholder");
  _placeholder.style.display = "none";
}
```

10. Add the following function, which sets the display message:

```
function ShowMessage()
{
    var _placeholder = document.getElementById("new_placeholder");

    if(_placeholder != null)
    {
      var _newDiv = document.createElement("div"); //
      style='overflow-y:auto; height:80px; border:1px
      #6699cc solid; background-color:#ffffff;' />");
      _newDiv.id = 'divMessage';
      _newDiv.innerHTML = "<label style='font-family:
      arial;color:red;font-size:20px'>Field Message must
      be set to No to be able to save the form!</label>";
      _placeholder.style.display = "none";
      var _previous = _placeholder.firstChild;
      if(_previous == null)
      {
        if(_placeholder.childNodes.length == 0)
        {
          _placeholder.parentNode.appendChild(_newDiv);
        }
        else
        {
          _placeholder.insertBefore(_newDiv, _previous);
        }
      }
      else
      {
        _placeholder.replaceChild(_newDiv, _previous);
      }
    }
}
```

11. Add a base function that does the processing and determines when to show the message, and possibly, other logic:

```
function message(context)
{
  var _isMessage = Xrm.Page.getAttribute
  ("new_message").getValue();
  if(_isMessage)
  {
    ShowMessage();
    // other logic here
  }
}
```

12. Save and publish your web resource.

13. In the **Contact** main form properties, associate the `contactLoad` function to the form `OnOpen` event.

14. Also on the **Contact** main form associate the function message to the `OnSave` event. You can alternatively associate this function at a field level if you want to do field validation and bring a message for invalid field value.

15. Save and publish your solution.

16. Test your solution. The result will look similar to the following screenshot:

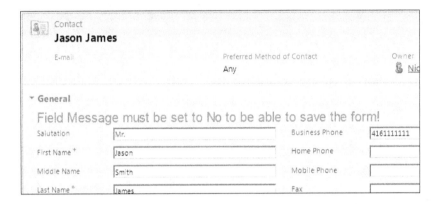

How it works...

As mentioned previously, this customization falls in the unsupported category. The reason is that objects are accessed using standard HTML/JavaScript DOM and not the Dynamics CRM API. Although unsupported, this kind of customization has been used since previous versions of Dynamics CRM, and as long as the HMTL/JavaScript standards are being supported, it will work.

There's more...

Message location is something you can easily determine by positioning your **Placeholder** field on the form at any location. For the purpose of this example, we have positioned the message at the top of the form, but that is not a mandatory location. Also, we have defined the placeholder to span the whole width of the page. You can decide to show the message only in one column if you desire so.

See also

▶ Additional information on Document Object Model can be found by starting from the wiki page located at `http://en.wikipedia.org/wiki/Document_Object_Model`.

- w3schools has a good tutorial on using JavaScript to navigate the DOM in an XML file at `http://www.w3schools.com/dom/dom_nodes_navigate.asp`. For all intended purposes, HTML is following the standard XML format, thus making these same scenarios available when working with HMTL, XHTLM, and XML.

- Additional information on traversing the DOM can be found in W3C located at `http://www.w3.org/wiki/Traversing_the_DOM`.

Advanced error handling

While the basics of any good development practice include error trapping and handling, when using JavaScript with Dynamics CRM 2011 your options revolve around using the try/catch block in a creative way. But the standard catch block has some additional features you should be taking advantage of when needed.

Getting ready

For this exercise we will be either using an existing solution or creating a new one. We will be creating a script that shows all available error-handling options available to us when using JavaScript with Dynamics CRM.

How to do it...

For advanced error handling perform the following steps:

1. Open your existing solution or create a new one.
2. Add the **Contact** entity to your solution.
3. Create a new **Two Options** field named **Error Handling** (new_errorhandling). Leave the standard **Yes** and **No** options.
4. Add the field to the form.
5. Save and publish the form.
6. Create a new JScript web resource named **JS Error Handling** (new_JSErrorHandling).
7. Add the following function to your script resource:

```
function myErrorHandling()
{
  // put in code that generates an error
  // change this code to throw various error types
  // and see how the errors are being captured
  try
  {
    throw new URIError("This is a URIError thrown...");
```

```
      // throw new RangeError("This is a RangeError thrown...");
      // throw new TypeError("This is a TypeError thrown...");
      // throw new SyntaxError("This is a SyntaxError thrown...");
      // throw new Error("This is a Custom Error thrown...");
    }
    catch(err)
    {
      switch(err.name)
      {
        case "URIError":
          alert(err.name + " || " + err.message);
        break;
        case "RangeError":
          alert(err.name + " || " + err.message);
        case "TypeError":
          alert(err.name + " || " + err.message);
        break;
        case "SyntaxError":
          alert(err.name + " || " + err.message);
        break;
        case "CustomError":
          alert(err.name + " || " + err.message);
        break;
      }
    }
    finally
    {
      alert("This block executes at all times");
    }
  }
```

8. Save and publish the resource.

9. Associate the function we just created to the `OnChange` event of our **JS Error Handling** form field.

10. Save and publish your solution.

11. Test the solution by setting the value of **JS Error Handling** to **Yes**. The script will execute, and will prompt alerts based on the type of error encountered, as well as a final message generated by the block.

12. Change the main block of code to generate other type of errors as described in a previous recipe, and observe the various errors handled in this function.

How it works...

This function processes a block of code that is meant to throw an error. The type of error in our example is the standard-type error, but you can change the kind of error thrown by looking at the *Handling unexpected processing* recipe. We are catching various types of errors that JavaScript can return, and performing various functions based on that. For this example, we are only returning different alert messages, but you can decide to build additional code to massage the form or process additional calculations as needed. In the end, we add a final block, which will execute no matter what kind of error we captured. This demonstrates ways of identifying the type of error generated by your code, and decide which way to handle it.

For the sake of simplicity our function does not check the value of the field that generates the OnChange event.

Adding a new account and contact with validation

In this recipe, while the use of scripting is suppressed, we are implementing logic to perform a duplicate detection validation when inserting a new account. The purpose of this recipe is to demonstrate that we can force a user to choose if he/she wants to create a duplicate or not from the get go, rather than relying on a duplicate detection job to run. This approach still uses the system-defined duplicate detection rules, but makes the process dynamic and interactive for the user.

You can easily implement the same functionality for contacts, or you can merge both checks in the same process.

Getting ready

Either create a new solution or use the previously created solution. This recipe will work with dialog processes, and will create a more detailed process to qualify a lead.

How to do it...

To add a new account and contact with validation perform the following steps:

1. In your solution, add a new process of type **Dialog**. The associated entity is **Lead**. Give this process a name of **Qualify Lead**. Make it available to run on demand.

2. Add a first stage named **Choose Entity Stage**, by going to **Add Step** and then selecting **Stage**, as shown in the following screenshot:

3. Inside this stage add a new page named **Select Entities to create**.

4. Inside this page, add a prompt and response. Name it **Contact**.

5. Set its properties, as described in the following screenshot:

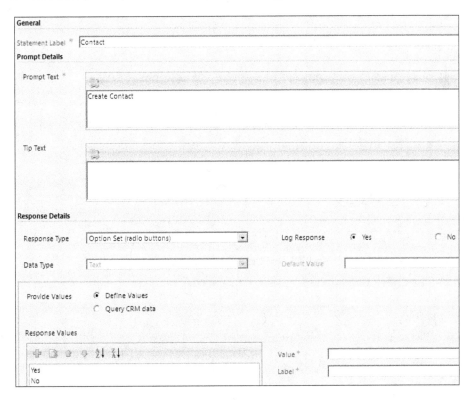

6. Add another prompt and response. Name it **Account**.

7. Set its properties, as described in the following screenshot:

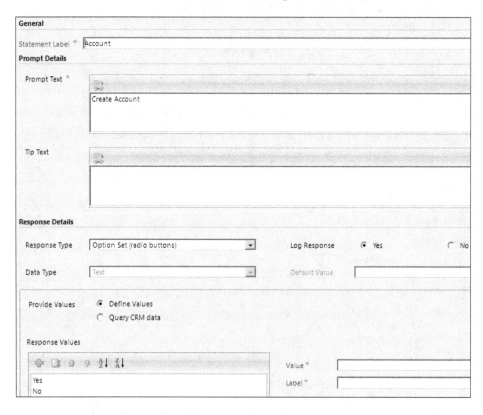

8. Add a new stage. Name it **Check Create Contact Stage**.

9. Add a **Check Condition** step. Set the rule, as follows:

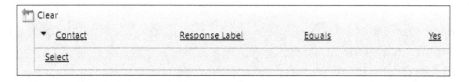

10. Within this condition, add a **Query CRM Data** step. Name it **Query CRM for Contacts with email matching the Lead**.

11. Set the query properties, as follows:

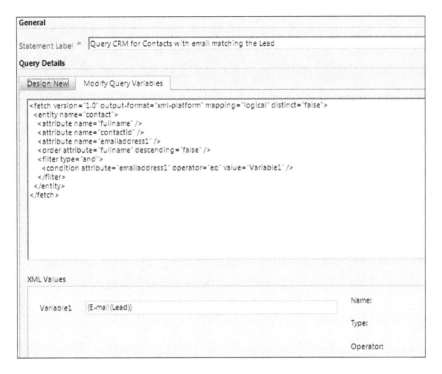

12. Add a **Check Condition** step. Label it **No matching Contact records**. Set the condition, as follows:

13. Add within this condition a **Create Record** step to create a new contact.

14. Also add within this same condition an **Update Record** step to update the Lead customer.

15. Add a **Conditional Branch** step to step 12.

16. Add a new page; label it **One or more duplicate Contacts found**.

17. Add on this page a prompt and response, as follows:

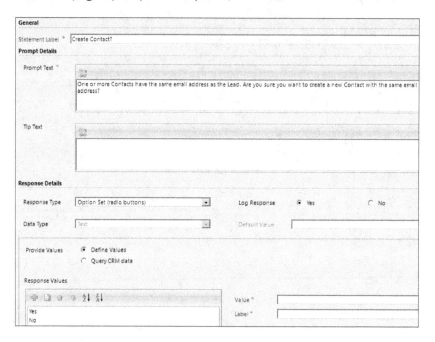

18. Add another prompt and response to this page, and define them as follows:

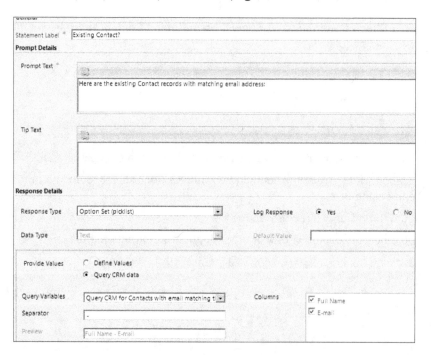

19. At the same level with the last page added in step 16 add a new **Check Condition** step. Set the condition, as follows:

20. Within this condition defined previously add a new **Create** step to create a new contact.
21. Also create an **Update** step to update the Lead customer.
22. For the condition in step 19 add a conditional branch.
23. Within the branch add a new **Update** step to update the Lead customer.
24. Create a similar process we used from steps 8 to 23 to create the contact. This time we will apply it to the **Account** entity.

 If you want to create only a contact from a Lead, you can skip steps 6 and 7.

25. Lastly, create a new stage to finalize our process. In this stage we will create the opportunity, mark **Lead** as **Qualified**, and add a **Stop Dialog** step. It should all look like the following screenshot:

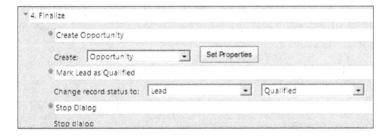

26. Save and activate this process. If any errors are returned, fix those errors and activate again.
27. Create a new Lead and run this dialog manually. Eventually, you can create a ribbon button to start this process, but we will demonstrate that in another chapter.

How it works...

The process itself does not have a complex logic. Instead of running the standard Lead qualification process, we start this dialog. It prompts the user if he/she wants to create **Account** and **Contact** based on the lead information.

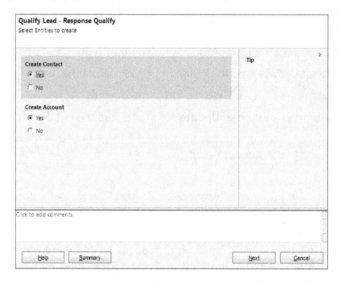

The user selects none, one, or both and clicks on **Next**. For each entity to be created it then checks if other contacts or accounts exists in the system with similar properties. If they don't, it creates new ones. If they do, it brings a list of possible matches to choose from, as shown in the following screenshots:

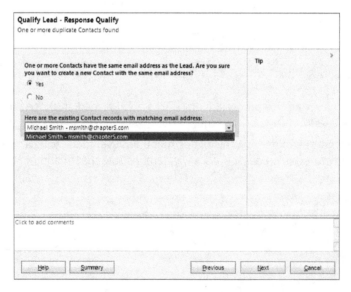

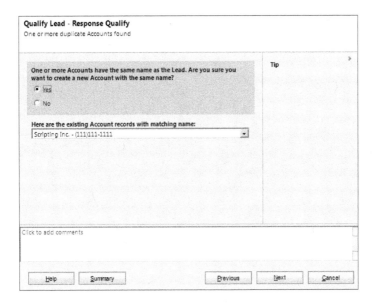

Once you have defined new or existing **Account** and **Contact** details, the process marks **Lead** as **Qualified** and opens an opportunity.

6
Debugging

In this chapter, we will cover:

- ▶ Debug messages
- ▶ Using IE for tracing and debugging
- ▶ Debugging using Visual Studio
- ▶ Error logging
- ▶ Using Fiddler with CRM

Introduction

As we start working with various scripts to customize our Dynamics CRM 2011 environment, we soon realize that we're not perfect, and we make mistakes. We've looked at handling errors dynamically in previous chapters. This time we will take a closer look at debugging. We are faced with various options for debugging. Each person is different, and each will have a different style of working with code. One thing is for sure though, at some point or another we all need to debug our code.

This chapter presents various ways of debugging. For some of the scenarios, we don't need anything more than a browser. For other scenarios we present tools that might come with a price tag. Most developers will have access to these, but if you don't, it's safe to skip those particular sections.

Debug messages

All modern browsers will prompt you when your scripts are not correct. The problem is, sometimes, these messages are not necessarily the most accurate or correct. For that reason we create debug messages at certain key points in our code that can be returned. This way we can easily identify what part of our code has executed, and where we are getting stuck.

JavaScript makes a few methods available to us, some more helpful than the others in certain situations, to insert our own custom debug messages.

One option we have seen before in some of the scripts we worked on already is using an **alert**. This brings up a pop-up message for the user. This approach, while easy to follow, is quite disruptive if we are testing a longer script, as we will have to click on OK on each message individually. By the time we have our fifteenth message up, we can safely say it's not the preferred approach. Especially if we run the same script multiple times until we can finally figure out what causes our error.

Another approach, a little less disruptive one, is to use an **assert statement**. In order for us to trace the messages returned that way, we can easily take advantage of the built-in browser's JavaScript console.

Finally, we can create our custom function to log all the messages. In conjunction with a `try... catch... finally` block, we can display all the processed messages in a single alert. This is a more desirable approach when working with long loops or when a multitude of messages are returned.

So now, let's explore these options in a short script.

Getting ready

We can either use one of the previously created solution packages, or we can create a new one for this chapter.

How to do it...

For the purpose of this recipe, we'll be focusing again on the **Contact** entity, so let's add it to our solution.

1. Add the **Contact** entity to your solution.
2. Create a new JScript resource and name it `JS Debug Messages` (`new_jsdebugmessages`).

3. Add a function that we will execute when the form is saved. Name it DebugSelector. This function looks at the selected value in an option set, and decides what other functions to call.

```
function DebugSelector()
{
  var sval = Xrm.Page.getAttribute("new_debugoptions").
getSelectedOption().text;
  var message = "Selected option is: " + sval;

  switch(sval)
  {
    case "Alert":
      CallAlert(message);
    break;
    case "Assert":
      CallAssert(message);
    break;
    case "Custom":
      CallCustom(message);
    break;
  }
}
```

4. Add the following function to work with alert messages:

```
function CallAlert(msg)
{
  alert(msg);
}
```

5. Also, add the following function to work with assert statements:

```
function CallAssert(msg)
{
  console.assert(false, msg);
}
```

6. And finally, add the following function to work with a custom way of collecting all messages into a single alert message:

```
function CallCustom(msg)
{
  var _message = msg;
  // some code
  _message = _message + "Another generated message. ";
  // additional code
```

```
    _message = _message + "Yet another message. ";
    // finally at the end of the script
    alert(_message);
}
```

7. **Save** and **Publish** our JScript web resource.

8. Now that we have our scripts together, let's add a new option set to the **Contact** entity. Name it `Debug Options (new_debugoptions)` and add the following three values:

   - ❏ Alert
   - ❏ Assert
   - ❏ Custom

9. On the field's `OnChange` event, associate the `DebugSelector()` function.

10. **Save** and **Publish** your customizations.

11. Open up a **Contact** and select **Alert** on the **Debug Options** option set. You will be presented with a regular pop-up message as shown in the following screenshot:

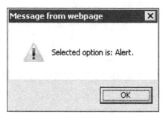

12. Next, open up the developer tools by pressing the *F12* key in Internet Explorer and navigate to the **Console** tab. Then go and change the **Debug Options** selection to **Assert**. You will get the messages in the **Console** windows as shown in the following screenshot:

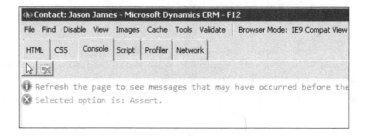

13. Finally, select the **Custom** option in the **Debug Options** option set. You will get a single pop up including all messages collected throughout the script. This might be the preferred approach if you are only collecting a small number of messages on iteration.

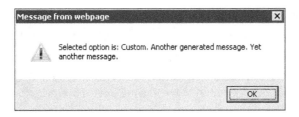

How it works...

When selecting the **Alert** option, the result is obvious to the user. Each alert statement returns a new pop-up message to the user.

When working with the **Custom** option, all messages are stored in a temporary variable, thus composing a single message to be presented to the user. At the end, this message is shown in a single pop up. While less intrusive, this approach can become non-desirable if the amount of messages or the length forces the pop-up message to be too large or trim content.

The last option is using the **Assert** option. While being the least intrusive, it does require a little bit of browser configuration. First off, in Internet Explorer, navigate to **Tools | Internet Options**. On the **Advanced** tab, make sure the **Display a notification about every script error** checkbox is selected. Also uncheck the **Disable script debugging** options.

Then, open the **Developer Tools** in IE by either clicking on the *F12* key, or navigating to **Tools | F12 developer tools**. Select the **Script** tab and look at the console while executing your page scripts.

There's more...

In addition to using the `assert` statement to log messages to the console, you can also use any of the following statements:

```
console.log("your message");
console.info("your message");
console.warn("your message");
console.error("your message");
```

Using IE for tracing and debugging

While writing our JScript code, it is highly unlikely that we will always get it right. We could, of course, start throwing alerts and any other type of notifications. The disadvantage to that is the fact that, once we fix the problem, we have to spend the time to go back and clean up the code.

In this recipe we'll be looking at alternative ways to trace our small mistakes.

Getting ready

For the purpose of this recipe, we will not be writing any new code. We'll be using the solution created in the *Handling unexpected processing* recipe in *Chapter 5, Error Handling*, and we will be tracing through the execution of those scripts using Internet Explorer and the Developer Tools.

How to do it...

First off, in order to use the Developer Tools in Internet Explorer, we need to make sure that script debugging is enabled. As mentioned at the end of the previous recipe, in Internet Options, on the **Advanced** tab, make sure that **Disable script debugging (Internet Explorer)** and **Disable script debugging (Other)** are not checked.

To open the Developer Toolbar, hit the *F12* key or go to **Tools | Developer Tools** on the page you want to debug.

For script debugging, go to the **Script** tab. Select the **new_JSErrors** script from the scripts dropdown. Click on the **Start debugging** button and place a breakpoint at the line you want to start your debugging from. Now that you have your debug point set, execute a form action that will kick off the script you are debugging. For example, if you have an action that is performed as a result of changing a lookup value, put your breakpoint at the beginning of that script, and then change the lookup value to kick off your script.

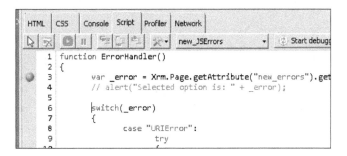

Once your script execution reached the breakpoint, you can start debugging from there in the same way you would debug any application on Visual Studio.

Another way to set breakpoints on specific scripts is by selecting the dropdown to the left-hand side of the **Start debugging** button, and selecting a specific script source.

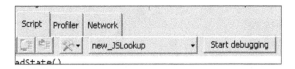

Another aspect of debugging using the Developer Tools in Internet Explorer involves the **Console**. Here you can watch for error messages. If the page generates an error message, in the **Console** window you will see the message. Clicking on the message link will put the focus in the script window on the line that generates the error.

The other tabs present additional functionality.

The **Breakpoints** tab includes a listing of all the breakpoints you have set up in your scripts.

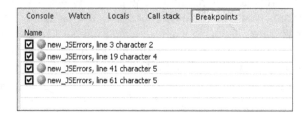

The **Watch** window allows you to define specific variables used during your script, and to see the allocated value at a certain point during execution. When using the **Watch** window, you can add the watched variables one by one, manually.

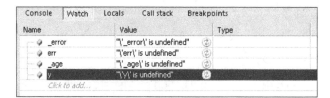

As you work and become more familiar with using this tool, you will see the added value and the speed benefits when debugging this way rather than using simple alerts.

How it works...

The Developer Tools in Internet Explorer, while not specific for Dynamics CRM, adds additional value to your toolbox. This tool is intended to be used in debugging any web application. We have only looked at the script portion of this tool, but it can add more value using the full range of options. You can easily debug all kinds of web resources you add to the pages, all scripts, and it provides additional help when investigating performance issues.

See also

▶ For additional details on getting started and using the Developer Tools in Internet Explorer, see the MSDN documentation at `http://msdn.microsoft.com/en-us/library/ie/gg589500(v=vs.85).aspx`.

Debugging using Visual Studio

While debugging using the Internet Explorer Developer Tool provides additional features for our efforts, developers have another option too. We can use Visual Studio for debugging in the same manner used for any other custom application. You will find this approach preferred when debugging custom plugins, but it is not limited to that.

Getting ready

In order to provide an example of using Visual Studio for debugging, we'll be using one of the existing solutions we created earlier in our recipes. In addition, in order to capture actual errors, add some intentional errors to your scripts.

How to do it...

The process of setting up Visual Studio for debugging is as follows:

1. Insert the following debugger line in your JScript code where you want to start debugging:

   ```
   debugger;
   ```

 Please note that using this also works in debugging using Internet Explorer.

2. Make sure the **Disable script debugging** option is unchecked in **Internet Options** as described previously.

3. When Internet Explorer hits the debug point, it will ask you how you want to debug your code.

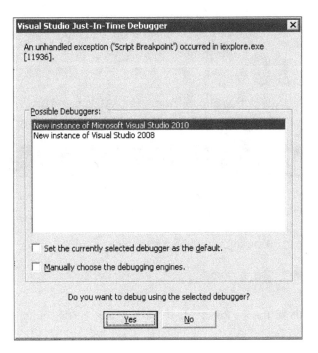

4. Once you click **Yes**, Visual Studio opens at the line where you inserted your debugger statement.

```
new_JSContact [dynamic]  ⊕  ✕
      function ReadBusinessPhone()
      {
        var myBusinessPhone;
        myBusinessPhone = Xrm.Page.getAttribute("telephone1").getValue();
        alert("You have entered: " + myBusinessPhone);
      }

      function IsSpecialCustomer()
      {
              debugger;
        var _isSpecialSelection = null;
        var _isSpecial = Xrm.Page.getAttribute("new_isspecialcustomer");

        if(_isSpecial != null)
        {
          _isSpecialSelection = _isSpecial.getValue();
        }
```

 From here on you can debug using the same principles of Visual Studio you use on any other application, using the *F11* key to step into the code, and the *F10* key to step over specific blocks. Please note that using this works also in debugging using Internet Explorer.

The advantage of using this approach sits primarily with developers that are familiar with Visual Studio. You get a dynamic view of script variables and breakpoint sets.

How it works...

This debugging technique is not unique to Dynamics CRM. You can use Visual Studio to debug any kind of web application in this manner.

Error logging

Dynamics CRM 2011 does not provide a direct way to add and track your own custom error messages. While the default logs will track and log errors as they occur, sometimes it's not the easiest way to debug. In order for us simplify the task of debugging and logging your specific error messages, we can take a different approach.

Getting ready

For the purpose of this recipe we will create a new solution. Using your current environment, or a new online instance, create a solution called Chapter6. This solution will use the latest version of JSON and jQuery libraries.

How to do it...

Within the newly created solution, let's focus our attention on the **Account** entity. We will capture our debug and error messages generated by a script in this solution.

1. Add the **Account** entity to your solution.

2. When you add the **Account** entity, you will be prompted to include additional required components. Add those too.

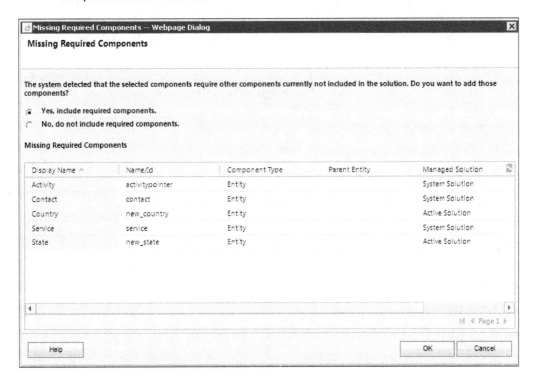

3. Add the most recent version of JSON 2 and jQuery libraries as web resource. Load the files by uploading them.

4. Add a new web resource of type JScript. Name it `Chapter 6 Error Logging` (`new_ch6errlog`).

5. Add the following two functions to it:

```
function LogOnLoadMessage()
{
  LogMessage("OnLoad Message", "This message is generated on
load", "Account");
}
```

```
function LogOnChangeNameMessage()
{
  LogMessage("OnChange Message - Name", "The Account Name has
changed", "Account");
}
```

6. Associate the `LogOnLoadMessage()` function with the `OnLoad` event of the **Account** form.

7. Associate the `LogOnChangeNameMessage()` function with the `OnChange` event of the **Name** field on the **Account** form.

8. On the **Account** form load, in the form libraries add the JSON 2 and jQuery libraries also.

9. In your solution add a new entity called `ErrorLog`. Set its ownership to **Organization**. Remove the checks on all the **Communication & Collaboration** options.

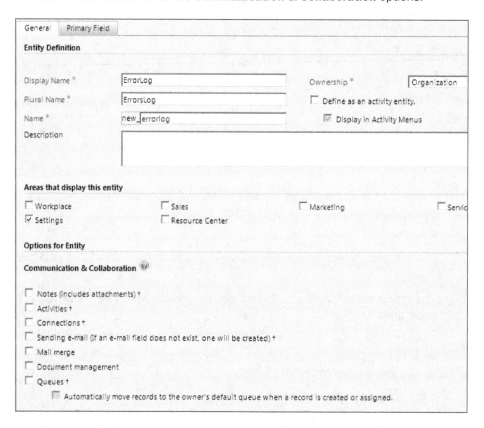

10. On the main form, in addition to the default **Name** field, add another two fields. One is named `Content (new_content)` as a multi-line text field, the other is `Entity (new_entity)` as a text field.

11. In your original web resource, add a function to be called on form load. This function calls another that builds the content of the message that will be logged in the new entity.

```
function LogOnLoadMessage()
{
  LogMessage("OnLoad Message", "This message is generated on
load", "Account");
}
```

12. In the same web resource, add another function that will be called when the name of the account changes.

```
function LogOnChangeNameMessage()
{
  LogMessage("OnChange Message - Name", "The Account Name has
changed", "Account");
}
```

13. Next, add a function that builds all these messages into an object that can be passed for writing.

```
function LogMessage(name, content, entity)
{
  var _message = new Object();
  _message.Name = name;
  _message.Content = content;
  _message.Entity = entity;
  createRecordAsync(_message);
}
```

14. On the last line of the previous function we call a new function that will do the actual writing using a SOAP message. The function looks as follows:

```
function createRecordAsync(message)
{
  var authenticationHeader = GenerateAuthenticationHeader();
```

```javascript
    // prepare the SOAP message
    var xml = "<?xml version='1.0' encoding='utf-8'?>" +
             "<soap:Envelope xmlns:soap='http://schemas.xmlsoap.
org/soap/envelope/'" +
             " xmlns:xsi='http://www.w3.org/2001/XMLSchema-
instance'" +
          " xmlns:xsd='http://www.w3.org/2001/XMLSchema'>" +
          authenticationHeader +
          "<soap:Body>" +
          "<Create xmlns='http://schemas.microsoft.com/crm/2007/
WebServices'>" +
      "<entity xsi:type='new_errorlog'>" +
      "<new_name>" + message.Name + "</new_name>" +
      "<new_content>" + message.Content + "</new_content>" +
      "<new_entity>" + message.Entity + "</new_entity>" +
      "</entity>" +
      "</Create>" +
      "</soap:Body>" +
      "</soap:Envelope>";
    //Prepare the xmlHttpObject and send the request
    var xHReq = new ActiveXObject("Msxml2.XMLHTTP");
    xHReq.Open("POST", "/mscrmservices/2007/CrmService.asmx",
false);
    xHReq.setRequestHeader("SOAPAction","http://schemas.microsoft.
com/crm/2007/WebServices/Create");
    xHReq.setRequestHeader("Content-Type", "text/xml;
charset=utf-8");
    xHReq.setRequestHeader("Content-Length", xml.length);
    xHReq.send(xml);
    // Capture the result
    var resultXml = xHReq.responseXML;

    // Check for errors.
    var errorCount = resultXml.selectNodes('//error').length;
    if (errorCount != 0)
    {
        var msg = resultXml.selectSingleNode('//description').
nodeTypedValue;
        alert(msg);
    }
    // Open new record if needed
    //else
    //{
    //    var contactid = resultXml.selectSingleNode("//
CreateResult");
```

```
    //    window.open("/sfa/conts/edit.aspx?id={"+contactid.
nodeTypedValue+"}");
    //}
}
```

15. Now go back to the **Account** form and associate the `LogOnLoadMessage()` function described in step 11 with the form `OnLoad` event.

16. In addition, associate the `LogOnChangeNameMessage` function with the `OnChange` event of the **Name** field on the **Account** form.

17. **Save** and **Publish** your solution.

18. Test your code by first loading an account.

19. Next, test the function by changing the name of the account.

20. In order to see the logged messages, either navigate to the **ErrorLog** view, or access the feed at `http://your_server_name/instance_name/XrmServices/2011/OrganizationData.svc/new_errorlogSet`.

21. If you are using an online instance use `http://your_instance_name.crm.dynamics.com/XrmServices/2011/OrganizationData.svc/new_errorlogSet`. What you will see is similar to the following screenshot:

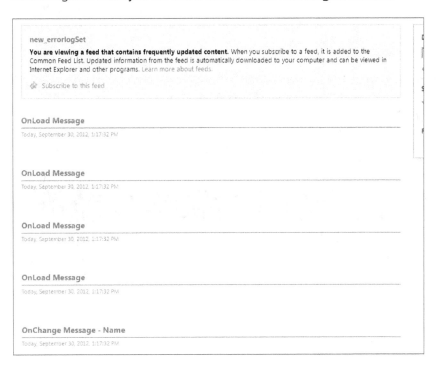

22. You will see all the messages logged along with the time when each message was generated.

How it works...

The previous approach presents the ability to use Microsoft CRM customizations through functional messages or new custom error entities. While this approach should not necessarily be used for any kind of generic error logging, as the number of messages can become quite large and hard to track, it shows you a different way of logging specific messages from your customization.

This approach can also be used in conjunction with the **audit log**, to allow you to capture specific actions of the user. It also provides great flexibility when it comes to implementing specific business rules and tracking when they are not strictly followed.

There's more...

While we have been investigating this approach for message logging, the same approach described in the function on step 14 can be used to add new records programmatically in any other system entity. This approach can be taken when you need to generate new addresses for **Account** or **Contact**, but do not want to have the user navigate to another screen to achieve that. Additionally, your business rule can potentially require the creation of new records in related entities. This function will work with both custom and out-of-the-box entities.

See also

- For additional details on using SOAP to create new entities in Dynamics CRM, look at the documentation on MSDN at `http://msdn.microsoft.com/en-us/library/cc677070.aspx`.

- In addition to that, Dynamics CRM allows you to perform other actions programmatically as well. See the additional documentation on MSDN at `http://msdn.microsoft.com/en-us/library/cc150864.aspx`.

Using Fiddler with CRM

Fiddler is a web debugger tool. It logs all web traffic (`http` and `https`) between your browser and a server. You can use it to inspect the requests and responses between your browser and any web application. For the purpose of this recipe, we will be focusing our attention on the communication between Internet Explorer and our Dynamics CRM server. You can use Fiddler even when using a development machine running Dynamics CRM.

Other advantages of using Fiddler include the ability to set breakpoints and obtain details surrounding performance issues.

Getting ready

To begin this recipe, we need a Dynamics CRM server, a user account on Dynamics CRM, as well as Fiddler installed.

You can download Fiddler from the web for free at `http://www.fiddler2.com`.

How to do it...

1. Once you have Fiddler installed, let's launch the application. The main screen looks like the following screenshot:

2. You will observe on the main screen, on the left-hand side, the captured requests or responses, while the right-hand side includes the standard welcome message.

3. On the ribbon, click on **Browse** to open Internet Explorer.

4. Navigate to your Dynamics CRM environment.

5. Once the page loads, let's go back to Fiddler and see what was captured.

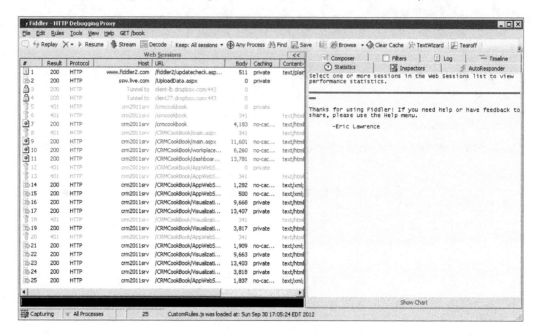

6. What we have here is a listing of the calls to our host machine, and the Dynamics CRM application pages and scripts requested.

7. Click on each one of the lines. Observe additional details displayed on the right-hand side window in the **Statistics** tab. These include performance counters.

This view will give you pretty detailed indications as to how much data is being sent both ways with a page request, as well as how long it takes to render a page requested from the server. This is fairly important information when you are trying to debug performance issues.

8. The **Inspectors** tab allows you to analyze the **Request** and **Response** headers.

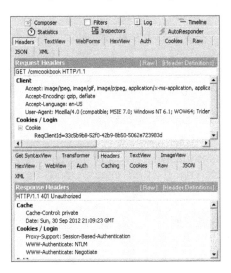

9. This ability to inspect web service requests and responses helps us to actually track requests like the one presented in the previous recipe. The example we just looked at will present the following information:

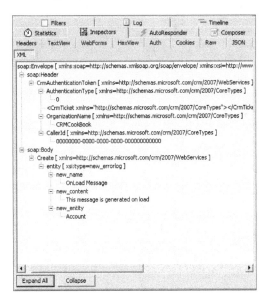

10. From here we can see the data we are sending to create a new error log record. The response is also presented as follows:

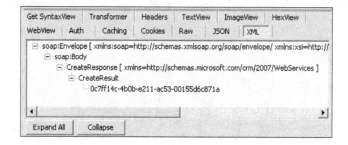

11. From here we can see the ID of the record that was just created.

12. In order to see the request and the result, make sure the **XML** button is clicked.

13. In addition, we can also inspect the JScript functions we have created. We can look at any of the calls referencing a web resource, and at the response we see the script called for.

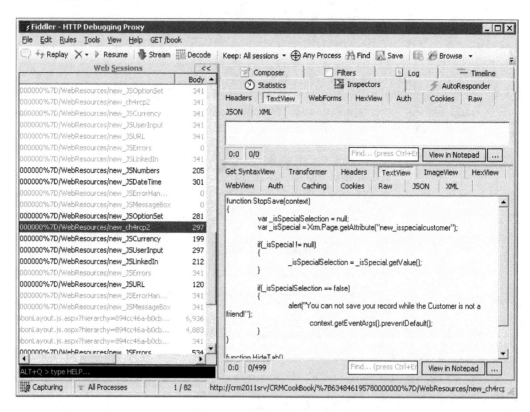

How it works...

Fiddler allows us to investigate different aspects of the communication from the browser to the web application and back. From inspecting scripts to looking at SOAP calls, as well as investigating performance issues, this tool should not be missing from your toolbox.

 Please note that when using Fiddler you cannot trace calls made to "localhost". You would have to connect from a remote machine.

See also

► To download Fiddler, and to find additional information and tutorials, head to the Fiddler site at `http://www.fiddler2.com/fiddler2/`.

7
Extended UI Manipulation

In this chapter, we will cover:

- ► Showing or hiding form elements
- ► Formatting fields
- ► Creating a rating gauge field
- ► Flagging a section for the user
- ► Adding a contact picture
- ► Adding an account logo
- ► Marking accounts for review
- ► Dynamic form elements

Introduction

This chapter will review some of the concepts covered previously, and introduce you to some advanced ways of manipulating the user interface. We will be focusing mostly on user experience by creating a few recipes in which we will hide and show various parts of the form; we will work with pictures and other ways of presenting and flagging specific information to the users.

This chapter assumes that the reader has a prior knowledge of customizing Dynamics CRM, yet is completely independent of the previous recipes in this book.

Showing or hiding form elements

In this recipe, we will focus on making the form as user friendly as possible. We can achieve this by showing specific fields only when required, and hiding irrelevant form elements when they are not required. We can work at various levels, where we can affect an individual field, a whole section, or a tab. Attention should be paid to how we group elements on the form, as this could potentially result in unexpected results, and a form layout that is not appealing to users.

Getting ready

For this recipe, make sure you have access to a Dynamics CRM 2011 environment. You must have a system customizer or system administrator permission in that environment to implement these customizations. Do not do these exercises in a production environment.

How to do it...

As we have previously seen in the recipes of *Chapter 2, Scripting Form Fields*, working with a specific field is probably the easiest way to begin this. This recipe will help you create the following scenario: on the **Contact** entity, we will capture a contact type of *staff*, *member*, or *non-member*. If the selection is *staff*, we will show a **Staff Details** tab. If the selection is *non-member*, we will show a **Non-Member Details** section, and if the selection is *member*, we will show only a **Member Number** field on the form. So, let's begin!

1. Create a new solution.
2. Add the **Contact** entity to your solution if not already added.
3. Open the main **Contact** form for editing.
4. Add a new field called `Contact Type`. Make it an **Option Set**. Add the following three values:
    -   `Staff`
    -   `Member`
    -   `Non-Member`
5. Add the field to the **Contact** form.
6. Add a new tab to the form. Change its label to `Staff Details` and its name to `tab_staff_details`.
7. On the **General** tab, add a new two-column section. Change its name to `non_member_section`. Change its label to `Non-Member Section` and check the **Show a line at top of the section** checkbox.

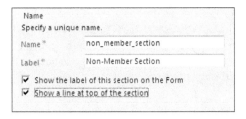

8. In the **General** section, add a new field called `Member Number`. Make it a single-line text field.

9. **Save** and **Publish** the form. We will return to it once we have the script completed.

10. In your solution, add a new web resource. Name it `JS Membership` (`new_jsmembership`) and make it of type **Script (JScript)**.

11. Add the following script to your resource:

```
function MembershipUI()
{
    var _selectedOption = "";

    try
    {
        _selectedOption = Xrm.Page.getAttribute("new_contacttype").
getSelectedOption().text;
    }
    catch(err)
    {}

    switch (_selectedOption)
    {
    case "Staff":
     // show Staff Details tab
       Xrm.Page.ui.tabs.get("tab_staff_details").setVisible(true);
       Xrm.Page.ui.tabs.get(1).sections.get(4).setVisible(false);
       Xrm.Page.ui.controls.get("new_membernumber").
       setVisible(false);
    break;
    case "Member":
     // show Member Number field
       Xrm.Page.ui.tabs.get("tab_staff_details").setVisible(false);
       Xrm.Page.ui.tabs.get(1).sections.get(4).setVisible(false);
       Xrm.Page.ui.controls.get("new_membernumber").
       setVisible(true);
    break;
    case "Non-Member":
```

```
       // show Non-Member Details section
       Xrm.Page.ui.tabs.get("tab_staff_details").setVisible(false);
       Xrm.Page.ui.tabs.get(1).sections.get(4).setVisible(true);
       Xrm.Page.ui.controls.get("new_membernumber").
        setVisible(false);
     break;
     default:
      // hide all
       Xrm.Page.ui.tabs.get("tab_staff_details").setVisible(false);
       Xrm.Page.ui.tabs.get(1).sections.get(4).setVisible(false);
       Xrm.Page.ui.controls.get("new_membernumber").
        setVisible(false);
   }
 }
```

12. Associate this function to the OnChange event of the **Contact Type** field.

13. **Save** and **Publish** your solution.

14. Test by selecting different values for the **Contact Type** option set.

How it works...

The preceding function reads first the selected option on the **Contact Type** field. Once this value is retrieved, it checks to see which of the three values is selected, and shows or hides the relevant form element/elements. We are demonstrating the process to hide/show a form tab, a form section, and a single field in this recipe.

See also

▸   Additional information on working with tabs can be found in MSDN at
    http://msdn.microsoft.com/en-us/library/gg328067.aspx.

▸   Additional details on working with sections is on MSDN at
    http://msdn.microsoft.com/en-us/library/gg328489.aspx.

Formatting fields

This recipe will show you how to format a text field in the xxx-xxx-xxx format. We have seen in previous recipes how to format phone numbers, or postal codes; this process is similar.

Getting ready

In the previously used solution, we will format the **Member Number** field to show as the previously mentioned format.

How to do it...

1. In the previously created web resource called **JS Membership (new_jsmembership)**, add the following script:

```
function FormatMemberNumber()
{
    var _mNumber = Xrm.Page.getAttribute("new_membernumber").
getValue();
    _mNumber = _mNumber.replace("-","");
    if(_mNumber.length == 9)
    {
        var _formattedNumber = _mNumber.substring(0,3) + "-" +
            _mNumber.substring(3,6) + "-" +
            _mNumber.substring(6,9);
        Xrm.Page.getAttribute("new_membernumber").setValue(_
          formattedNumber.toString());
    }
    else
    {
Xrm.Page.getAttribute("new_membernumber").setValue("");
    }
}
```

2. Associate this function to the `OnChange` event of the **Member Number** field.

3. Test by inserting various strings in that field. Make sure that the field re-formats your input to respect the standard format, or clears your field if the input is incorrect.

How it works...

This function reads the user input when the focus is lost, and parses this input trying to format it as per the requirement. It removes any dashes in the string, and checks to make sure the remaining length is 9 characters. If the length is anything but 9, it clears the field. If it is 9, then it formats the string by adding dashes back where required and populates the text field with the formatted value.

Creating a rating gauge field

In this recipe, we will be looking at presenting the status of a record in a pleasant and visual way. We are looking to provide instant feedback on the record based on a calculated or form-defined value. You could be using such an approach when marking accounts based on annual revenue or any other type of status. You could also use a more complex formula to determine an account worth and display that in a rating gauge on the **Account** form.

Getting ready

For this recipe, we can either reuse the previously created solution in the first two recipes of this chapter, or create a new one. Make sure you have the system customizer or system administrator permissions to the environment.

How to do it...

Let's follow these steps to add a rating gauge to the **Account** form:

1. Create three images. Depending on your graphics skills, you could go with something really complex, or just a simple colored dot, like I did in this example.

2. Load your three images as web resources in your solution. I have called them `red`, `yellow`, and `green`, all in the PNG format. Make a note of the URL.

    ```
    https://<ServerUrl>/WebResources/new_red
    https://<ServerUrl>/WebResources/new_yellow
    https://<ServerUrl>/WebResources/new_green
    ```

3. Open the main **Account** form for editing.

4. Select a location where you want the image displayed. You might want to move form elements around the page so that your image aligns nicely with the rest of the fields.

5. Insert a web resource on the form. On the **Add Web Resource** form, in the **Web resource** field, look-up the **new_green** image we have loaded previously. Your settings should look like the following screenshot:

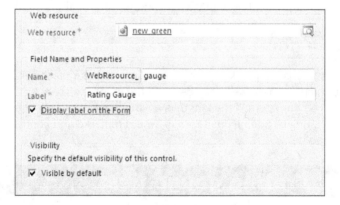

6. On the **Formatting** tab, in the **Row Layout** area, select the number of rows you want the image will occupy. I will change the default value to **7**. Leave the remaining settings as they are.

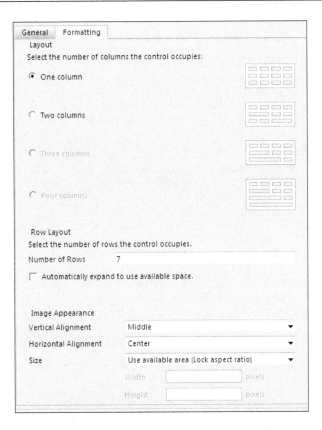

7. Add a new form field of type **Option Set** with three values of Red, Yellow, and Green. Name this field new_ratinggaugesource. Set the default value to Green.

8. Add the following script to your form, and attach it to the OnChange event of the new_ratinggaugesource field:

```
function RatingGaugeUpdate()
{
  var _selectedOption = "";

  try
  {
    _selectedOption = Xrm.Page.getAttribute("new_
ratinggaugesource").getSelectedOption().text;
  }
  catch(err)
  {}

  switch (_selectedOption)
  {
```

```
      case "Red":
          Xrm.Page.getControl("WebResource_gauge").setSrc (Xrm.Page.
      context.getServerUrl() + "/WebResources/new_red");
          break;
      case "Yellow":
          Xrm.Page.getControl("WebResource_gauge").setSrc Xrm.Page.
      context.getServerUrl() + "/WebResources/new_yellow");
          break;
      case "Green":
          Xrm.Page.getControl("WebResource_gauge").setSrc Xrm.Page.
      context.getServerUrl() + "/WebResources/new_green");
          break;
      }
  }
```

9. **Save** and **Publish** the solution.

10. Test your customization by opening a new account and changing the option set to any
    of the three values provided. Then try the others. The end result should be similar to
    the following screenshot:

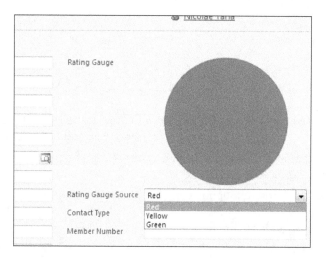

How it works...

The previous example shows us two important things. First off, we can add images to forms
if the images are stored as a web resource. This will be helpful when we need a few status
indicators. Next, it shows us how to replace that default image using JavaScript. For the
purpose of this example, we only take the user-selected value of a form option set and change
the image according to the selection. One of the following recipes will demonstrate how we
can extend this functionality to pull images dynamically from other external sources.

Flagging a section for the user

In this recipe, we will take a look at how to bring a section of the form to the attention of the user. We can do this for various reasons, whether we want to let the user know that a section is more important than the others, or simply to decorate our form.

Getting ready

We can either use one of the previously created solutions, or create a new solution. We will need to be either a system administrator or a system customizer.

How to do it...

Perform the following steps to highlight a section to the user by changing the background color of that section. We will be using the **Account** entity for this customization, and we will create a new section. We could do the same on an existing section.

1. Open the solution, or create a new one.
2. Add the **Account** entity to the solution if not already added.
3. Open the main **Account** form for editing.
4. Add a new section to the form. Configure it as per the following screenshot:

5. Add some fields to this section.
6. **Save** and **Publish** this form.

7. Add to your solution a new web resource named `new_JSAccount`. Make it of type **Script (JScript)**.

8. Add the following function to your web resource:

```
function HighlightSection()
{
    document.getElementById("{be295314-4459-5e75-68de-
81921170754b}").style.backgroundColor = '#CD0000';
}
```

9. **Save** and **Publish** the web resource.

10. On the main form of the account, attach the function to the `OnLoad` event of the form.

11. **Save** and **Publish** your solution.

12. Test it by opening a new account. You should see the section highlighted with a background colored in red as shown in the following screenshot:

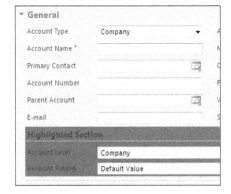

How it works...

While this is an unsupported customization, it's been available since previous versions of Dynamics CRM, and it's still an easy and comfortable way of handling user-interface changes.

The line of code in our function gets a reference to the section, and applies a background-color style formatting. We can easily get the internal ID of the section by using the Internet Explorer Developer Tools console. We have focused on using the Developer Tools in our debugging section in *Chapter 6, Debugging*.

There's more...

There are some additional ways to interact with the user interface. Some of them involve the use of other external libraries, such as jQuery. We will be looking at how to use jQuery in *Chapter 9, Extending CRM Using Community JavaScript Libraries*.

Adding a contact picture

Based on some of the previous examples, this recipe shows a very basic way to reference a contact picture from an external source. This source could be anything from an internal repository to any public image hosting site. Also, you can use the same approach to load images to any entity. In the following recipes, we will delve deeper into referencing images from within the system.

Getting ready

For this example, we will be using an existing solution. Alternatively, we can create a new solution. We will customize the **Contact** entity.

How to do it...

1. Add the **Contact** entity to your solution if not already added.

2. Add a new web resource of type **JScript**.

3. Add the following function to your entity:

```
function AddContactPicture()
{
    var _imageURL = Xrm.Page.getAttribute("new_profileimage").
getValue();
    Xrm.Page.getControl("WebResource_ContactPicture").setSrc(_
imageURL);
}
```

4. Open the main **Contact** form for editing.

5. Add a new **Web Resource** element to your form. Name it `WebResource_ContactPicture`.

6. In the **Web resource** lookup, point to a generic image as a base, in case no user image is provided.

7. Format it, so it looks right on the **Contact** form, by using the configurations on the **Formatting** tab.

8. Add a new **Text** field to the form, and format it as a **URL**. Name it `new_profileimage`.

9. Attach the `AddContactPicture()` function to the `OnChange` event of the previously created text field, as well as to the `OnLoad` event of the form.

10. **Save and Close** the form.

11. **Publish** your solution.

12. Test it by opening a new contact. On the first load, since no image URL is defined, the default image will be shown.

13. Add a URL to an image hosted on a public site.

14. Save the form. This will cause a form refresh. The image we've defined in the URL will now show in the image form element.

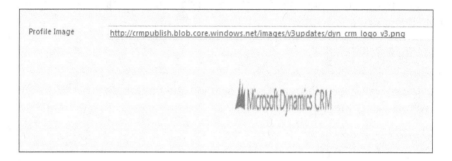

How it works...

The defined script loads a URL to an image and places that image in our form-defined web control. Formatting the text field as **URL** adds the necessary validation on the field, so we don't end up with unexpected user input.

There's more...

While using an image from an external source is quite easy using this approach, it's not necessarily a good idea to take this approach. You could consider keeping the image with the record. Take a look at the next recipe for an example on how to do that.

Adding an account logo

In this recipe, we will be looking at a simple way to allow users to add an account picture. We will create the form elements, and will load the picture from an attachment to the **Account** in the **Notes** area. For the purpose of this recipe, we will be expecting the logo to be named `account_logo.jpg`.

Getting ready

For this recipe, we can either create a new solution, or reuse one of the existing ones. Make sure you have the proper permissions to customize the system you work on. Add the **Account** entity to your solution.

How to do it...

1. Open the main **Account** form for editing.

2. Add a new **Web Resource** element to your form. Name it `WebResource_AccountLogo`. Add a label of `Account Logo`.

3. In the **Web resource** lookup, point to a generic image loaded as a web resource. This can be a generic default logo image.

4. The final screen should look like the following screenshot:

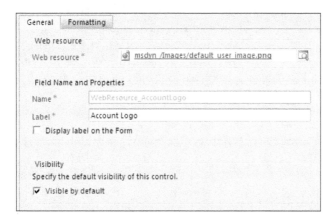

5. On the **Formatting** tab, set its properties such that it has one column, two rows, a vertical alignment of *top*, horizontal alignment of *right*, and of the *original size*. If you select *original size*, make sure that you parse the logos you are loading through an application that resizes them to a standard maximum width or height.

6. **Save** and **Publish** the form.

7. Create a new web resource within the solution, of type **JScript**.

8. Add the following functions:

```
function ShowContactPicture()
{
  var _contactId = Xrm.Page.data.entity.getId();
  if(_contactId)
  {
    var _pictureControl = Xrm.Page.getControl("WebResource_
AccountLogo");
    var _query = getServerUrl() + "/XRMServices/2011/
OrganizationData.svc/" +
"AnnotationSet?$top=1&$select=AnnotationId,DocumentBody,MimeType&"
+
          "$orderby=ModifiedOn desc&$filter=ObjectId/Id eq
guid'" + _contactId +
```

```
                          "' and IsDocument eq true and Subject eq 'Logo'" +
                          " and startswith(MimeType,'image/') ";

         $.ajax({
                    type: "GET",
                    contentType: "application/json; charset=utf-8",
                    datatype: "json",
                    url: _query,
                    beforeSend: function (request) { request.
         setRequestHeader("Accept", "application/json"); },
                    success: function (data, textStatus, request) {
                         if (data.d.results.length > 0) {
                              var mimeType = data.d.results[0].MimeType;
                              var body = data.d.results[0].DocumentBody;
                              _pictureControl.setSrc("data:" + mimeType +
         ";base64," + body);
                         }
                    },
                    error: function (request, status, exception) { }
              });
         }
    }


    function getServerUrl()
    {
      var serverUrl = Xrm.Page.context.getServerUrl();
      return serverUrl.replace(/\/*$/, "");
    }
```

9. Associate the `ShowContactPicture()` function to the form `OnLoad` event.

10. Open a new account, and add a new note by navigating to **Add** and then clicking on **Add Note**.

11. In the window that opens, fill in the title as `Logo`, and browse to a logo file.

12. Click on **Attach**.

13. Click on **Save and Close**.

14. Now your logo file will be added to the account in the **Notes** area.

15. Refresh the page to force the script to execute. You should see something similar to the following screenshot:

How it works...

The function presented first retrieves the ID of the current account. Once a valid non-null value is retrieved, it takes a reference to the picture control, it queries **Notes** for a note with the **Title** of `Logo`, and it retrieves the image field attached. It then parses the image and associates it to the web resource control we have already added to the page, thus making it render on the form.

There's more...

There is a large variety of sources you can use for images. You can either store the image in **Notes** as this example demonstrates, or you can store images as web resources if the users maintaining accounts have permission to add new web resources. Alternatively, you can use any of the public online photo services, and link to the images at those locations. There is also the option of leveraging any of the current social networking services, but we will look at that in a later chapter.

See also

> ▶ This recipe has shown you code that leverages two very popular libraries: jQuery and JSON (`json2.js`). *Chapter 9, Extending CRM Using Community JavaScript Libraries*, will delve deeper into this topic, but for now, you can find the libraries at the following URLs:

> > ❑ `http://jquery.com/download/`
> > ❑ `http://www.json.org/`

Marking accounts for review

Sometimes we need to flag an account to make it obvious to the user that some action needs to take place. This recipe will show you two ways to do that. First off, we will put a different border color around the form. Secondly, we will add a colored title to the form, including a message to the user.

Getting ready

For the purpose of this exercise, we can reuse an existing solution. If none exists, create one. Make sure that you have at least the system customizer permission.

How to do it...

Open the solution and perform the following tasks:

1. Add the **Account** entity to your solution if not already added.

2. If asked to add related entities, click on **Yes**.

3. Open the main **Account** form for editing.

4. Add a new text field named `new_opencases` with a label of `Open Cases`. Place the field on the form.

5. **Save** and **Publish** the form.

6. Add the jQuery resource as described in previous recipes.

7. Add a new web resource of type **JScript**. Name it `new_JSAccount`.

8. Add the following script to your resource:

```
function ChangeBorderColor()
{
  var _cases;
  try
  {
  _cases = parseInt(Xrm.Page.getAttribute("new_opencases").
getValue());
  }
  catch(err)
  {
    _cases = 9999;
  }

  if(_cases < 10)
  {
    // set border green
    $(".ms-crm-Form-Page-Main-cell").css("background-
color","#00FF00");
  }
  elseif(_cases < 20 && _cases >= 10)
  {
    // set border yellow
    $(".ms-crm-Form-Page-Main-cell").css("background-
color","#FFFF00");
  }
  else
  {
    // set border red
```

```
    $(".ms-crm-Form-Page-Main-cell").css("background-
color","#FF0000");
    }
}
```

9. Associate the script to the form's `OnLoad` and the `new_opencases` field's `OnChange` events.

10. **Save** and **Publish** the solution.

11. Test your customization by loading an account. Modify the value of open cases in the field.

 In *Chapter 9, Extending CRM Using Community JavaScript Libraries*, we will demonstrate how to populate the **Open Cases** field automatically, taking advantage of external libraries.

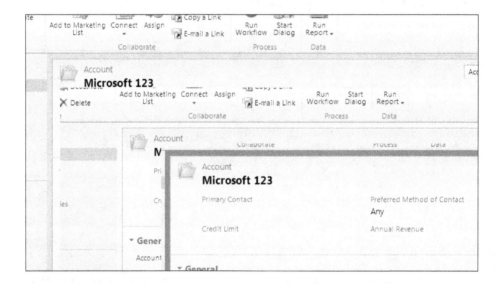

How it works...

Based on the value stored in our **Open Cases** field, we determine specific thresholds on number of open cases per account. This way we flag an account status to the user by providing a different color to the form border. In this example we are taking advantage of the jQuery library to select the form border, and to set the `background-colour` CSS property.

The following chapter will delve deeper into using the jQuery library for various form element selections, as well as other nifty tricks.

▶ Additional details on the jQuery library can be found in *Chapter 8, Working with Ribbon Elements*, as well as on the jQuery page, at `http://jquery.com/`. The documentation is located at `http://docs.jquery.com/`.

Dynamic form elements

There comes a time when the standard controls offered by Dynamics CRM are not enough to satisfy the user's requirements. One such example is if they need to select multiple items in a field. While this can be done by generating a section with multiple checkboxes, what if the user wants a more elegant solution? Something along the lines of a multi-select dropdown?

In addition, the solution presented here allows, in a very easy way, to report on those selections in an easy-to-read format.

In this recipe, we will be looking at a way to create a control that allows the multi-select functionality to the user. While this is an unsupported customization, it's been the de facto way of doing this for the last few years, and it's been working flawlessly.

Getting ready

For this recipe, we can either reuse an existing solution or create a new one. Please make sure you have at least the system customizer permission in the environment you will be using. This code works in both Online and On-Premise environments of Dynamics CRM 2011.

How to do it...

In order to prepare our work area, let's start by creating a few basic elements on the form. In this example I want to capture food preferences for a contact.

1. Create a new solution.

2. Add the **Contact** entity to your solution.

3. Open the main **Contact** form for editing.

4. Add a new section on the form to host your control. Alternatively, you could add a new tab with a default section if you want a shortcut on the navigation tree.

5. Within this new section, add an option set. Name it `new_optionset` and set a display name of `Preferred Food`. This display name will show on the form in front of the new multi-select field we'll create.

6. Since I am capturing food preferences in this example, add to the option set a list of food choices.

7. Also within this section, add a new text field. Name it `new_selectedvalues`. Set a display name of `Preferred Food` also. This field will be hidden on the form, but we will display it in a summary view.

8. Place your fields on the form in the section created. Your form should now look like the following:

9. **Save** and **Publish** your form. We will come back to it later to attach the scripts, but for now we have all we need here.

10. Close the form and return to the solution.

11. Add a new web resource of type **JScript**. Name it `new_multiselect` with a display name of `Multi Select`. Try to keep descriptive names so it's easier to find them later when you have many web resources.

12. We will need to add three functions to this resource. First off, let's add the function that will be called when the form is loaded. This function prepares the form elements for the user, and looks up previously selected values.

```
function FormLoad()
{
    var _optionSet = document.all.new_optionset;
    var _optionSetValues = document.all.new_selectedvalues;
    Xrm.Page.ui.controls.get('new_selectedvalues').
setVisible(false);
    document.all.item("new_optionset").style.display = "none";

    var addDiv = document.createElement("<div style='overflow-
y:inherit;'/>");
  _optionSet.parentNode.appendChild(addDiv);
  for( var i = 0; i < _optionSet.length; i++ )
  {
    var _option = _optionSet.options[i];
    if(_option.text != "") {
      // create the checkbox
```

```
        var _style = " style='border:none; width:30px;
align:left;'";
        if(!IsOptionChecked( _option.text, _optionSetValues))
        {
          var _checkBox = document.createElement("<input
type='checkbox'" + _style + " />" );
        }
        else
        {
          var _checkBox = document.createElement("<input
type='checkbox' checked='checked'" + _style + " />" );
        }
        // create the checkbox label
        var _label = document.createElement("<label>" + _option.text
+ "</label>");
        _label.innerText = _option.text;

        _optionSet.nextSibling.appendChild(_checkBox);
        _optionSet.nextSibling.appendChild(_label);
_optionSet.nextSibling.appendChild(document.createElement(
"<br/>"));
      }
   }
}
```

13. Next, let's add the function that executes when the form is saved. This function reads the user-populated checkboxes and adds the values to the hidden text field we've created.

```
function FormSave()
{
  var _optionSet = document.all.new_optionset;
    var getInput = _optionSet.nextSibling.
getElementsByTagName("input");
    var result = "";
    for( var i = 0; i < getInput.length; i++ )
    {
    if(getInput[i].checked)
    {
      result = result + getInput[i].nextSibling.innerText + ";";
    }
    }
Xrm.Page.getControl("new_selectedvalues").getAttribute().
setValue(result);
}
```

14. And lastly, we need a small helper function that looks through the values stored in the text field and compares them against the value we are checking.

```
function IsOptionChecked( _optionText, _optionSetValues)
{
    var _string = _optionSetValues.defaultValue;
    if(_string != "")
    {
      var _arr = _string.split(";");
      for(var i = 0; i < _arr.length; i++)
      {
        if(_arr[i] == _optionText)
          return true;
      }
    }
    return false;
}
```

15. With our three functions added, let's **Save** and **Publish** the web resource, then close it.

16. Now let's return to the form we customized in step 7. Open the form for edit again. This time go to **Form Properties** on the **Events** tab and load your form library. Next, in the **Event Handlers** section, add the `FormLoad()` function to the `OnLoad` event of the form, and the `FormSave()` function to the `OnSave` event of the form.

17. **Save** the form, and **Publish** your solution.

18. Now we can test our customization. Open a new contact. On your form you will see something similar to the following:

19. Initially, no options will be selected. Select a few choices, and click on the **Save and Close** button. Reopen it, and your choices are all saved.

20. The beauty of this solution also stretches beyond the simple form customization. You can easily create a simple view that will show you the food preferences of any contact in the system. It can look like the following:

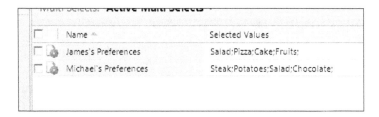

How it works...

The principle is twofold here:

When we open the form, we look into the hidden text field to see if there are any saved values. If present, then we check the boxes accordingly.

When we close the form, we read all the selections on the screen, we clear the hidden text field, and we repopulate it with the currently selected values. Remember, use the labels, then populate the text field and you will see them nicely in the view.

The reason this type of customization is not supported is because it steps outside of the recommended object model, and it uses the standard JavaScript and HTML DOM.

8
Working with Ribbon Elements

In this chapter, we will cover:

- ▸ Adding a new ribbon button
- ▸ Removing ribbon artefacts
- ▸ Starting a dialog/workflow from a ribbon button
- ▸ Pre-populating form elements with a button click
- ▸ Creating other ribbon artefacts
- ▸ Security trimmed ribbon elements
- ▸ Using the ribbon for displaying information

Introduction

This chapter focuses on working with the ribbon and elements contained within it. We will start with small steps in adding a simple button and proceed into more advanced topics around actions and customizations. We will close this chapter with an example of using the ribbon as a container for elements other than buttons.

Working with the ribbon elements involves working with a lot of XML. For references on XML see the *See Also* section of the first recipe.

 Errors in customizing the ribbon elements can result in the element to be added being not displaying at all, or even making the whole ribbon non-functional. Please do your testing in an environment where you are not affecting any other processes, and most importantly, do not try to do this directly in a production environment.

Adding a new ribbon button

This recipe will start you with the basics. We'll be looking at adding a new ribbon button. Be aware that you can add a ribbon button across all entities or to a specific entity only. Read through the steps, as there are points identifying which action has to be taken and when.

The ribbon is comprised of the following elements:

- **Tabs**
- **Groups**
- **Controls**

Each of these elements are stacked one inside the other. Tabs contain Groups that contain Controls.

In order to customize the ribbon, please be aware that there are various levels at which this customization can be implemented. These levels are as follows:

- Ribbon at the web application level
- Ribbon at the form level
- Ribbon at the grid level
- Ribbon at the entity level

In addition to these levels, we can also customize the Outlook ribbon.

Getting ready

Use an existing instance of Dynamics CRM, or create a new one if one is not available. Make sure you have at least the system customizer permission in order to be able to perform the following customizations.

How to do it...

Perform the following steps to add a new ribbon button at the web application level.

1. Create a new solution. Name it `RibbonCustomization`. Select a **Publisher** or create a new one and add a version number.
2. Save the newly created solution.
3. Once saved, click on **Components**.
4. Click on **Add Existing** and select **Application Ribbons**.
5. **Save** and **Publish** your solution.
6. Export the solution and create a backup of it.

7. Extract the files from the solution. The solution is a ZIP file.

8. Open `customizations.xml` for editing.

9. Find the `<RibbonDiffXml>` section.

10. Find the `<CustomActions>` tag inside.

11. Add a new `<CustomAction>` tag, give it an `Id`, a `Location` and a `Sequence`. The `Id` has to be unique, the `Location` defines the ribbon section, and the `Sequence` defines the order in that specific ribbon section. More details about each attribute can be found in MSDN at the link in the _See also_ section at the bottom of this recipe.

12. Add a new `<CommandUIDefinition>` tag.

13. Now go to the CRM SDK and find the `applicationribbon.xml`. It is located in the `/sdk/resources/exportedribbonxml/` folder.

14. Find a `<Button>` definition and copy it. Replace `Mscrm` with `CRMScripting`.

15. Paste it in the `<CommandUIDefinition>` tag.

16. The following is a sample of how this section could look like:

```
<CustomActions>
<CustomAction Id="CRMScripting.MyCRM.MainTab.LaunchURL.
CustomAction"
Location="Mscrm.HomepageGrid.MyCRM.MainTab.Actions.Controls._
children"
      Sequence="80">
<CommandUIDefinition>
<Button Id="CRMScripting.MyCRM.MainTab.LaunchURL.Button"
Command="CRMScripting.all.MainTab.LauchURL.Command"
      LabelText="Qualify"
         ToolTipTitle="Qualify Button"
         ToolTipDescription="Click to see the Demo Button
functionality"
         TemplateAlias="o1"
Image16by16="$webresource:new_/my16Button.png"
Image32by32="$webresource:new_/my32Button.png" />
      </CommandUIDefinition>
    </CustomAction>
  </CustomActions>
```

17. Next, find the `<CommandDefinitions>` tag.

18. Add a `<CommandDefinition>` tag to it.

19. Then add the following code:

```
<CommandDefinitions>
  <CommandDefinition>
     <EnableRules />
     <DisplayRules />
```

```
            <JavaScriptFunction Library="$webresource:jsbook.js"
                FunctionName="LaunchNew" />
        </CommandDefinition>
    </CommandDefinitions>
```

20. Save and re-package the solution.

21. Add a new **JScript** web resource and add the following function to it:

```
function launchNew()
{
alert("From within launchNew JS function!");
}
```

22. Create two new images of 16 x 16 pixels and 32 x 32 pixels.

23. Load them as web resources. Name them `my16Button.png` and `my32Button.png`.

24. Now re-load the original solution you have pulled out.

25. **Save** and **Publish** your customizations.

26. You will now see a new button added to the ribbon as shown in the following screenshot:

How it works...

There are two steps to this customization. First off, we modify the XML definition by adding the button to the `customizations.xml` file. There we have the references to the images and the JavaScript function that is called when the button is clicked.

Second, we add the JavaScript function to open a pop-up window when the button is clicked. A variety of actions can be taken from here.

There's more...

This generic example showed how to add a new ribbon button to the application ribbon which is displayed in all entities, but as we mentioned at the beginning, we have more choices here.

Adding a ribbon button to a specific entity

For the purpose of this example, let's focus on the **Lead** entity.

1. Find in the SDK the `leadribbon.xml` file at `...\sdk\resources\exportedribbonxml`.

2. Find the `<Ribbon>` tag within this file.

3. Find the `MainTab` section.

4. Identify the group you want to place your new button into and copy the control ID for one of the other controls in that group. In this case, I want to place the new **Qualify** button in the **Actions** group.

   `Mscrm.Form.lead.MainTab.Actions.Controls`

5. Add a new button definition, as described previously, and re-package and publish the solution.

6. Add the related JavaScript functions and the images as described.

7. **Save** and **Publish** all changes.

8. Test your changes by opening a new **Lead** entity. Your new button should show on the **Lead** ribbon.

See also

▶ For additional details on the XML elements, see the MSDN documentation at `http://msdn.microsoft.com/en-us/library/gg327915.aspx`.

Removing ribbon artefacts

Now that we have seen how to add a new ribbon button, how about we look at how to remove buttons? There will be instances where you will want to replace a standard out-of-the box button with a new custom one, or hide functionality from the user.

Getting ready

For this recipe, use the solution created in the *Adding a new ribbon button* recipe, or create a new one. Make sure you have the proper permissions to make these kind of customizations. You need to be a system administrator or a system customizer.

How to do it...

Perform the following steps to hide the **Qualify** button on the **Lead** entity:

1. Make sure you have the CRM SDK downloaded. If you don't have it, get the latest version.

2. Create a new solution package, or open the previously created one.

3. Add the **Lead** entity to your solution.

4. Export the solution and save it locally.

5. Unzip the solution package and remember the location.

6. Open the `customizations.xml` file for editing. Find the `Lead` section in the XML file.

7. Find the `<RibbonDiffXml>` tag within the `Lead` definition.

8. Change the `<CustomActions>` tag to read as the following:

```
<CustomActions >
<HideCustomAction Location="Mscrm.HomepageGrid.lead.ConvertLead"
HideActionId="Mscrm.HomepageGrid.lead.ConvertLead.HideAction" />
<HideCustomAction Location="Mscrm.Form.lead.ConvertLead"
HideActionId="Mscrm.Form.lead.ConvertLead.HideAction" />
</CustomActions>
```

9. Re-package your solution (zip it) and import it.

10. **Save** and **Publish** all customizations.

11. Refresh the browser to see the changes. You will observe the button disappear in the following places:

    1. **Lead** home page (before and after your customizations are applied).

2. **Lead** entity (before and after your customizations are applied).

How it works...

The approach in this example is pretty simplistic. All we are doing is adding a `HideCustomAction` property to the button. Observe on the two lines declared that we are, in fact, hiding the same button from the ribbon on both the **Lead** homepage and the **Lead** form.

See also

▶ For a description of all the ribbon elements see the documentation on MSDN at `http://msdn.microsoft.com/en-us/library/gg327947.aspx`.

Starting a dialog/workflow from a ribbon button

Now that we know how to hide a ribbon button and how to add our custom buttons to the forms, the next step is to make these buttons do something a little more intelligent than just bring up a pop-up message.

Getting ready

For the purpose of this recipe, we can either continue on the customizations started in the *Adding a new ribbon button* recipe at the beginning of this chapter, or re-create the button and the action as described there.

How to do it...

In order to kick off a workflow using a ribbon button, perform the following steps:

1. Add your new form button as described in the first recipe of this chapter.

2. Create your custom workflow as part of the same solution.

 We will require the workflow ID in our function. For the sake of simplicity, I will show you how to find out this ID manually and hard code it into your JavaScript function.

3. Start the workflow manually.

4. Go to **System Jobs** and find the job running the workflow.

5. Do a copy link. Paste that link into Notepad. You will see the following at the end of the link:

   ```
   id=%7b[GUID]%7d
   ```

   Where [GUID] is of the format XXXXXXXX-XXXX-XXXX-XXXX-XXXXXXXXXXXX.

6. Copy that GUID, as we will need it as a parameter in our JScript function.

7. Add a new JScript web resource that contains our function.

8. Add the following JScript function to our web resource:

   ```
   function launchWorkflow(dialogID, typeName, recordId)
   {
   // Load modal
   var serverUri = Xrm.Page.context.getServerUrl() + "/cs/dialog/
   rundialog.aspx";
    window.showModalDialog(serverUri + '?DialogId=' + dialogID +
   '&EntityName=' + typeName +
   '&ObjectId=' + recordId, null, 'width=615,height=480,resizable=1,s
   tatus=1,scrollbars=1');
   // Reload form
    window.location.reload(true);
   }
   ```

9. Export your solution to a location on your machine.

10. Unzip the solution file and remember the location.

11. Edit the `customizations.xml` file within the unzipped solution.

12. Find the `Lead` entity section.

13. Find the `RibbonDiffXml` section within the `Lead` tag.

14. Find the ribbon button definition, and within it find the `Actions` segment.

15. Replace the **Actions** with the following XML code:

```
<Actions>
 <JavaScriptFunction Library="$webresource:Nav_JS_Common_Lib"
FunctionName="launchWorkflow">
 <!- workflowId, entityName, entityId ->
 <StringParameter Value="{e1037cac-756c-46e7-96d0-cdc572eafc65}"
/>
 <StringParameter Value="lead" />
 <CrmParameter Value="FirstPrimaryItemId" />
 </JavaScriptFunction>
</Actions>
```

16. **Save** and **Publish** your solution.

17. Test it by creating a new **Lead** and clicking the new ribbon button.

How it works...

The solution presented is comprised of the following main actions:

1. Create a system workflow.
2. Add a new ribbon button.
3. Define the ribbon button action through JScript to point it to the custom workflow created.

Within the `customizations.xml` file, the following tags are important:

- `CustomActions`: It allows us to define the location of where the ribbon button appears.

- `CommandUIDefinition`: It is a container control that defines user interface elements along with properties such as `label`, `tooltip`, and `icon`.

- `CommandDefinition`: It defines the command to be executed.

- `Actions`: It allows us to customize the JScript function to execute or the URL to forward to. In this section we can also define parameters.

- `CrmParameter`: It permits us to pass information directly from the calling form. In our example we passed the GUID of the `Lead` record.

In order to process a workflow rather than a dialogue, we can use a similar approach, and point to the workflow ID. In addition, for more complex situations, we can launch workflows from a dialogue, or vice versa.

See also

 ▸ For additional details on parameters, see the MSDN documentation at
   `http://msdn.microsoft.com/en-us/library/gg309332.aspx`.

Pre-populating form elements with a button click

For this example, we will look at using a button click to populate form fields. We can use such a scenario when we need a calculation to take place on the form, or when we need to bring data from a related record. For example, we have a sub-account, and we need to bring and populate the address of the parent account. Automating this task will save the user a few minutes per record and will create a much better user experience.

Getting ready

For the purpose of this recipe, we can either use one of the pre-existing solutions, or create a new one. Make sure you have the proper permissions to allow you to customize the system as required. This example will work in both Online and On-Premise environments.

How to do it...

In order to create this functionality, perform the following steps:

1. Create a solution package in your environment or open an existing one.
2. Add the **Account** entity to your solution, if not already added.
3. Make sure you have a custom button image, or create a new one. Alternatively, you can use the default system image. For this example, I will use the default image.
4. Add a new web resource, of type **JScript**, and name it `new_getaddress`.
5. Within your web resource, add a function placeholder named `GetAddressFromParent`. We will come back to the function content after the button is added to the ribbon.
6. Export your solution from CRM.
7. Unzip the solution and remember the location.
8. Open the `customizations.xml` file for editing.
9. Find the **Account** entity section in the XML file.
10. Open up the SDK and find the **Account** XML file as described in the previous recipes (`accountribbon.xml`).

11. Find the section where you want to place your button. In this case, I want to place my custom button in the `Actions` section of the `Main` tab. So look for the tab defined with the following:

```
<Tab Id="Mscrm.Form.account.MainTab ...
```

12. Next, look for the following group definition:

```
Mscrm.Form.account.MainTab.Actions.Control
```

13. Back in our solution's `customizations.xml` file change the `CustomActions` section to look as follows:

```
<CustomActions>
 <CustomAction Id="OC.account.Form.Main.CustomAction"
Location="Mscrm.Form.account.MainTab.Actions.Controls._children"
Sequence="15" >
  <CommandUIDefinition>
   <Button Id="OC.account.Form.Main.Button"
       Command="OC.account.Form.Main.Command"
       LabelText="Copy Address"
       ToolTipTitle="Copy from Parent"
       ToolTipDescription="Copy Address from Parent Account"
       TemplateAlias="o1" />
  </CommandUIDefinition>
 </CustomAction>
</CustomActions>
```

14. If you were to add the button images, you would add the following two lines after `TemplateAlias`. You would add the two images to the solution as well.

```
Image16by16="$webresource:new_btn_16.png"
Image32by32="$webresource:new_btn_32.png"
```

15. Next, add the corresponding command definitions. Find the `CommandDefinitions` section, and change it to look as follows:

```
<CommandDefinitions>
 <CommandDefinition Id="OC.account.Form.Main.Command">
  <EnableRules>
  </EnableRules>
  <DisplayRules>
  </DisplayRules>
  <Actions>
   <JavaScriptFunction
    Library="$webresource:new_getaddress"
           FunctionName="GetAddressFromParent" />
  </Actions>
 </CommandDefinition>
</CommandDefinitions>
```

16. Save your changes and close the file.

17. Repack the solution as a ZIP file.

18. Reload the solution onto your environment.

19. If there are no errors on the import, then your customized package is correct.

 If you did not create the function placeholder beforehand, you will get an error on the import stating that your ribbon item is dependent on the web resource that holds your function.

20. You can now check and make sure that your button appears on the ribbon by opening a new or existing account record. Your button will show as follows if the images were not defined:

21. Next, open your function placeholder you have created earlier. At this point, create your function that retrieves the parent account's address, and populates the current address with that information. Your function could look like the following:

```
function GetAddressFromParent()
{
  try
  {
    var ParentAccount = Xrm.Page.getAttribute("parentaccountid");
    if(ParentAccount != null)
    {
      var ParentAccountValue = ParentAccount.getValue();
      if(ParentAccountValue != null)
      {
          var ParentAccountId = ParentAccountValue[0].id;

          var serverUrl = Xrm.Page.context.getServerUrl();
          var odataSelect = serverUrl + "/XRMServices/2011/
OrganizationData.svc/AccountSet(guid'" + ParentAccountId +
"')?$select=Name,Address1_Line1,Address1_Line2,Address1_
Line3,Address1_City,Address1_PostalCode";
```

```
        $.ajax({
                type: "GET",
                contentType: "application/json;
charset=utf-8",
                datatype: "json",
                url: odataSelect,
                beforeSend: function (XMLHttpRequest) {
XMLHttpRequest.setRequestHeader("Accept", "application/json"); },
                success: function (data, textStatus,
XmlHttpRequest) {
                        var org = data.d;
                        //Change form data
                        // alert("TEST: Country: " + org.
Address1_Country[0].name + "; Province: " + org.Address1_
StateOrProvince[0].name);
                        Xrm.Page.data.entity.attributes.
get("address1_name").setValue(org.Name);
                        Xrm.Page.data.entity.attributes.
get("address1_line1").setValue(org.Address1_Line1);
                        Xrm.Page.data.entity.attributes.
get("address1_line2").setValue(org.Address1_Line2);
                        Xrm.Page.data.entity.attributes.
get("address1_line3").setValue(org.Address1_Line3);
                        Xrm.Page.data.entity.attributes.
get("address1_city").setValue(org.Address1_City);
                        Xrm.Page.data.entity.attributes.
get("address1_postalcode").setValue(org.Address1_PostalCode);
                    },
                error: function (XmlHttpRequest, textStatus,
errorThrown) {
                        alert('OData Select Failed: ' +
odataSelect);
                    }
            }
        );
        }
      }
    }
  catch()
  {}
}
```

22. **Save** and **Publish** your solution.

23. Test it by opening an account, assigning a parent account, saving the record, and then clicking on your new custom button. You should see the address populated from the parent account.

How it works...

There are two major steps in this recipe we followed. First off, we add a ribbon button. While adding the button, we define the button properties as well as the associated function that is called when the button is clicked. Secondly, we define a custom function. This function requires the OData and JSON libraries. Do make sure that these libraries are added to your solution. The function presented retrieves the ID of the parent account, and makes a call to get some of the address properties of the parent account. Once this information is retrieved, it is populated into the current account address fields.

See also

- ▶ More information on the OData protocol can be found at `http://www.odata.org/`.

- ▶ OData JSON details are found at `http://www.odata.org/developers/protocols/json-format`.

Creating other ribbon artefacts

In this example, we will be looking at the flyout anchor ribbon element in Dynamics CRM 2011. This allows us to nest multiple ribbon buttons under a single header, thus saving space on the ribbon and grouping common elements together.

Getting ready

For this recipe, we can either use an existing solution, or create a new one. Make sure you have permissions to make customizations in the system.

How to do it...

Perform the following steps to generate a ribbon flyout that contains other buttons:

1. Create a new solution. Alternatively you can use any existing solution.
2. Add the **Account** entity if not already added. We will place the flyout on the **Account** ribbon.
3. Create and add two images for the flyout buttons of 16 x 16 and 32 x 32 pixels. Name them `flyout16.png` and `flyout32.png` respectively.
4. Alternatively, you can create additional images for the other submenu buttons. This example will reuse the same image for all buttons.
5. Load the images as web resources into your solution.
6. Add a new web resource of type **JScript**. Name it `new_flyoutfunction`.

7. Add the following function to your resource. This is the function that is called from the second ribbon button:

```
function flyoutaction()
{
    alert("You have run a function from a custom flyout ribbon
button...");
}
```

8. **Save** and **Publish** your solution.

9. Export your solution.

10. Unzip the solution.

11. Open the `customizations.xml` file for edit.

12. In the **Account** form ribbon add a new custom action.

 If we want to add this to the home page grid to display it on the listing of all accounts, we can change in the `Location` definition from `Mscrm.Form` to `Mscrm.HomePageGrid`.

The code could look as follows:

```
<CustomAction Id="OC.account.Button1.Button.CustomAction"
Location="Mscrm.Form.account.MainTab.Actions.Controls._children"
Sequence="29" >
  <CommandUIDefinition>
    <FlyoutAnchor Id="MyFlyout"
          ToolTipTitle="My Flyout"
          LabelText="My Flyout"
          Sequence="80"
          Image16by16="$webresource:new_flyout16.png"
          Image32by32="$webresource:new_flyout32.png"
          TemplateAlias="o1">
      <Menu Id="MyMenu">
        <MenuSection Id="MyMenuSection"
              Title="My Custom Flyout"
              Sequence="15"
              DisplayMode="Menu32">
          <Controls Id="MyControls">
            <Button Id="MyButton1"
                  ToolTipTitle="MyButton1"
                ToolTipDescription="MyButton1"
                  LabelText="Open Bing"
                  Alt="My Button 1"
              Image16by16="$webresource:new_flyout16.png"
```

```
                        Image32by32="$webresource:new_flyout32.png"
                        TemplateAlias="isv"
                        Sequence="10"
                        Command="OC.Button1"
                />
                <Button Id="MyButton2"
                        ToolTipTitle="MyButton2"
                        ToolTipDescription="MyButton2"
                        LabelText="Run Function"
                        Alt="My Button 2"
                Image16by16="$webresource:new_flyout16.png"
                Image32by32="$webresource:new_flyout32.png"
                        TemplateAlias="isv"
                        Sequence="11"
                        Command="OC.Button2"
                />
              </Controls>
            </MenuSection>
          </Menu>
        </FlyoutAnchor>
      </CommandUIDefinition>
    </CustomAction>
```

13. Next step, we need to define the commands. One of these two commands will contain a reference to a JScript to be run, the other simply opens a URL.

14. Add the first command definition for the first button. This button will only open a new browser window and navigate to the predefined URL.

```
<CommandDefinition Id="OC.Button1">
  <EnableRules />
  <DisplayRules />
  <Actions>
    <Url Address="http://www.bing.com"
         PassParams="false"
         WinParams="height=200, width=400, toolbar=no,
menubar=no, location=no" />
  </Actions>
</CommandDefinition>
```

15. Now add the second command definition for the next button. This definition calls our JavaScript function when the button is clicked.

```
<CommandDefinition Id="OC.Button2">
  <EnableRules />
  <DisplayRules />
  <Actions>
```

```
    <JavaScriptFunction Library="$webresource:new_flyoutfunction"
        FunctionName="flyoutaction" />
    </Actions>
</CommandDefinition>
```

16. Once the command definitions are added, package your solution again.

17. Import your solution. If all is ok, your solution should update the system with no errors.

18. Publish all the changes.

19. Now test your customization by opening a new or an existing account. You should see on the ribbon a new flyout with two buttons underneath. Click on both and observe the result.

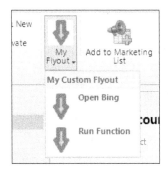

How it works...

There are three major steps to achieve this functionality.

First off, we need to define the parent control, the flyout anchor that will hold all the buttons on the ribbon.

Next step, we define the command definitions. We use two definitions; one for the first button demonstrating a standard way to open a pre-defined URL, and one for calling a function. With these two definitions we can further create more complex logic.

Finally, the script contains the function that is called when clicking the **Run Function** button.

See also

▶   For additional reference on the `FlyoutAnchor` see the MSDN documentation at http://msdn.microsoft.com/en-us/library/gg309511.aspx.

Security trimmed ribbon elements

In this recipe, we will be looking at dynamically removing a ribbon button when a certain condition is met. First off, we'll create a function to check for the condition. If the condition is met, a second function is called that hides an existing button. So let's get started.

Getting ready

For this recipe we can either use an existing solution, or create a new one. Make sure you have permissions to make customizations in the system.

How to do it...

For the sake of simplicity, we check to see if the current user is the owner of a contact, and if not, we hide the **Save** button. You can do the same with the **Save and Close** button, as well as any other ribbon buttons.

1. Create a new solution or open an existing one.

2. Add the **Contact** entity to your solution of not already added.

3. Add a new web resource of type **Jscript**.

4. Add the following function to check if the current user is the owner of the record:

```
function HideButtonIfNotOwner(context)
{
  var _currentUser = Xrm.Page.context.getUserId();
  var _formOwner;
  var _owner = Xrm.Page.getAttribute("ownerid");
  if(_owner != null)
  {
    var _ownerValue = _owner.getValue();
    if(_ownerValue != null)
    {
      var _formOwner = _ownerValue[0].id;
    }
  }
  if(_currentUser != _formOwner)
  {
    // hide ribbon button
HideButton("contact|NoRelationship|Form|Mscrm.Form.contact.Save-
Large"); // Save
  }
}
```

5. Observe the button name that is being passed to the `HideButton()` function. In order to retrieve the names of the buttons, use the Internet Explorer's Developer Tools. You can open it by pressing the *F12* key.

6. Next, add a new function that hides the button using the HTML DOM. Please note that while this is not an officially supported scenario, as long as the HTML DOM does not change, it's a simple way of doing this.

```
function HideButton(name)
{
  if(top.document.getElementById(name) != null)
  {
    var btn = top.document.getElementById(name);
    btn.style.display = 'none';
  }
}
```

7. Open the **Contact** form, and in the form properties, add the `HidebuttonIfNotOwner()` function to the `OnLoad` event.

8. **Save** and **Publish** your solution.

9. Test your customization by opening a record you own. You should see a **Save** button.

10. Next test it by opening a record where the owner is another system user. You should not see the **Save** button anymore.

How it works...

Our first function retrieves the ID of the current user, as well as the ID of the form owner. Comparing these values, it defines whether to call the next function or not. In our case, if the owner is not the same as the current user, we are calling the next function to hide the Save button. In order to make this functional, you should also hide the save & Close button, as well as the Save & New button. Alternatively, you can hide the whole Save ribbon tab.

Our next function takes advantage of the standard HTML DOM to find the document elements described by the passed IDs and defines the style properties to hide them.

There's more...

Same approach can be taken to hide ribbon tabs, not just buttons. Using the Developer Tools provided with Internet Explorer, you can find the ID of any form element, and hide it that way.

Enhancing the progression process of a record

While this example only looked at the owner of a record versus the current user, you can easily extend this kind of functionality to enhance the process of progressing a certain record through various phases. A combination of a new custom ribbon tab with buttons to progress from one stage to another, along with form validation that defines the current stage, and what buttons become available next is something relatively easy to accomplish now using the previous examples provided.

See also

- ▸ Information on HTLM DOM can be found at w3schools `http://www.w3schools.com/htmldom/default.asp`.

- ▸ Using JavaScript with HTML DOM is described also at w3schools `http://www.w3schools.com/jsref/default.asp`.

Using the ribbon for displaying information

In the *Creating a rating gauge field* recipe of *Chapter 7, Extended UI Manipulation*, we described a simple method to place a rating gauge on a form and changing the image based on a business rule. Similar to that, this time we will look at placing that rating gauge in the ribbon. The advantage to putting this kind of information on the ribbon is that it's always visible to the user no matter what section of the form you scroll to. So let's see how we can achieve this.

Getting ready

For this example we can use either an existing solution, or we can create a new one. Make sure you have permissions to make customizations to the system. We will add this to the **Account** entity.

How to do it...

Perform the following steps to add this functionality:

1. Create a new solution if one is not already available.

2. Add the **Account** entity to your solution if not already added.

3. Create three images to be used on the ribbon. I've made three circles, one red, one yellow, and one green.

4. Scale the three images at 16 x 16 pixels, as well as at 32 x 32 pixels.

5. Add your six images as web resources to your solution.

6. Add a new **JScript** web resource. Add a function placeholder as follows:

   ```
   function RibbonPlaceholder()
   {
       // empty placeholder
   }
   ```

7. Your listing of web resources should look like the following screenshot:

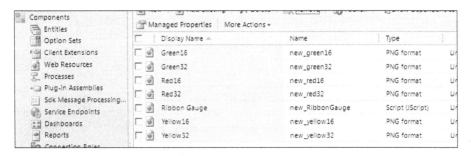

8. Export your solution as **Unmanaged**.

9. Unzip your solution.

10. Open the `customizations.xml` file for editing.

11. Find the `RibbonDiffXml` area within.

12. Add the following custom actions:

```
<CustomActions>
<CustomAction Id="OC.account.Form.Red.CustomAction"
Location="Mscrm.Form.account.MainTab.Actions.Controls._children"
Sequence="33">
<CommandUIDefinition>
<Button Id="OC.account.form.Red.Button" Command="OC.
account.form.Red.Command"
LabelText=" " ToolTipTitle=" " ToolTipDescription=" "
TemplateAlias="o3"
Image16by16="$webresource:new_red16"
Image32by32="$webresource:new_red32" />
</CommandUIDefinition>
</CustomAction>
<CustomAction Id="OC.account.Form.Yellow.CustomAction"
Location="Mscrm.Form.account.MainTab.Actions.Controls._children"
Sequence="34">
<CommandUIDefinition>
<Button Id="OC.account.form.Yellow.Button" Command="OC.
account.form.Yellow.Command"
LabelText=" " ToolTipTitle=" " ToolTipDescription=" "
TemplateAlias="o3"
Image16by16="$webresourcenew_yellow16"
Image32by32="$webresource:new_yellow32" />
</CommandUIDefinition>
</CustomAction>
<CustomAction Id="OC.account.Form.Green.CustomAction"
Location="Mscrm.Form.account.MainTab.Actions.Controls._children"
Sequence="35">
<CommandUIDefinition>
<Button Id="OC.account.form.Green.Button" Command="OC.
account.form.Green.Command"
LabelText=" " ToolTipTitle=" " ToolTipDescription=" "
TemplateAlias="o3"
Image16by16="$webresource:new_green16"
Image32by32="$webresource:new_green32" />
</CommandUIDefinition>
</CustomAction>
</CustomActions>
```

13. Next, find the command definitions and add the following code:

```
<CommandDefinition Id="OC.account.Form.Red.Command">
<EnableRules></EnableRules>
<DisplayRules></DisplayRules>
<Actions>
```

```
        <JavaScriptFunction Library="$webresource:new_
ribbongauge" FunctionName="RibbonPlaceholder" />
        </Actions>
    </CommandDefinition>
    <CommandDefinition Id="OC.account.Form.Yellow.Command">
        <EnableRules></EnableRules>
        <DisplayRules></DisplayRules>
        <Actions>
            <JavaScriptFunction Library="$webresource:new_
ribbongauge" FunctionName="RibbonPlaceholder" />
        </Actions>
    </CommandDefinition>
    <CommandDefinition Id="OC.account.Form.Green.Command">
        <EnableRules></EnableRules>
        <DisplayRules></DisplayRules>
        <Actions>
            <JavaScriptFunction Library="$webresource:new_
ribbongauge" FunctionName="RibbonPlaceholder" />
        </Actions>
    </CommandDefinition>
```

14. With that in place, re-package your solution.

15. Import your solution.

16. If all is correct, you will get a confirmation window. Click on **Publish All Customizations**.

17. Once you have your customized ribbon buttons published, open up an account to make sure all three buttons appear as expected in the ribbon. We will have a red circle, a yellow circle, and a green circle in our **Actions** section.

18. Observe that we have not defined a button name. While we placed the buttons in the **Actions** tab for this example, you can create your own custom tab or place them in any other available tab as needed.

19. Clicking any of the buttons on the ribbon will not result in any action. This is by design in this case, but the example shows a function associated with these buttons. You can add logic in that function to re-calculate the total that generates the field value that determines which flag is presented to the user.

20. In order so simplify this example, we will create an option set which will drive the ribbon-selection value. You can do this by adding more complex logic based on multiple form elements.

21. Add an option set named `new_ratinggauge`. Add three values to it, `Red`, `Yellow`, and `Green`.

22. Add the field to the **Account** form.

23. Add a new web resource named `new_jsratinggauge`. Set it of type **Script**.

24. Add the following function to your web resource to read the selection text:

```
function jsratinggauge()
{
  var _fieldValue = "";
  try
  {
  var _fieldValue = Xrm.Page.getAttribute("new_ratinggauge").
getSelectedOption().text;
  }
  catch(err)
  {
  }

  if(_fieldValue == "Red")
  {
    HideButtons("Red");
  }
  else if(_fieldValue == "Yellow")
  {
    HideButtons("Yellow");
  }
  else if(_fieldValue == "Green")
  {
    HideButtons("Green");
  }
  else
  {
    HideButtons("None");
  }
}
```

25. Once we have the selection text and we identify which action takes place, we call the following function, which hides the unnecessary ribbon buttons and only leaves the relevant one:

```
function HideButtons(validButton)
{
  if(validButton ==  "Red")
  {
    var btnRed = top.document.getElementById("account|NoRelationsh
ip|Form|OC.account.form.Red.Button-Large");
    btnRed.style.display = 'inline';
    var btnYellow = top.document.getElementById("account|NoRelatio
nship|Form|OC.account.form.Yellow.Button-Large");
    btnYellow.style.display = 'none';
    var btnGreen = top.document.getElementById("account|NoRelation
ship|Form|OC.account.form.Green.Button-Large");
    btnGreen.style.display = 'none';

  }
  else if(validButton == "Yellow")
  {
    var btnRed = top.document.getElementById("account|NoRelationsh
ip|Form|OC.account.form.Red.Button-Large");
    btnRed.style.display = 'none';
  var btnYellow = top.document.getElementById("account|NoRelations
hip|Form|OC.account.form.Yellow.Button-Large");
    btnYellow.style.display = 'inline';
    var btnGreen = top.document.getElementById("account|NoRelation
ship|Form|OC.account.form.Green.Button-Large");
    btnGreen.style.display = 'none';

  }
  else if(validButton == "Green")

    var btnRed = top.document.getElementById("account|NoRelationsh
ip|Form|OC.account.form.Red.Button-Large");
    btnRed.style.display = 'none';
    var btnYellow = top.document.getElementById("account|NoRelatio
nship|Form|OC.account.form.Yellow.Button-Large");
    btnYellow.style.display = 'none';
    var btnGreen = top.document.getElementById("account|NoRelation
ship|Form|OC.account.form.Green.Button-Large");
    btnGreen.style.display = 'inline';
  }
  else
```

```
{
    var btnRed = top.document.getElementById("account|NoRelationsh
ip|Form|OC.account.form.Red.Button-Large");
    btnRed.style.display = 'none';
    var btnYellow = top.document.getElementById("account|NoRelatio
nship|Form|OC.account.form.Yellow.Button-Large");
    btnYellow.style.display = 'none';
    var btnGreen = top.document.getElementById("account|NoRelation
ship|Form|OC.account.form.Green.Button-Large");
    btnGreen.style.display = 'none';
}
}
```

26. Associate the `jsratinggauge()` function to the `OnChange` event of the option set we created earlier. This will cause the ribbon to update dynamically once the selection changes.

27. Also associate the `jsratinggauge()` function to the form's `OnLoad` event. This way, when we open a new record, the gauge updates.

28. **Save** and **Publish** your solution.

29. To test the functionality, open an **Account** record. If no value is selected on the option set, no button is displayed on the ribbon.

30. Change the option set selection from one option to another and observe the ribbon getting updated to reflect the selected color. Your ribbon will look like the images shown in the following screenshot:

How it works...

The approach of this solution is similar to the way we customize a form. We add to the ribbon all the elements we use, and then, based on a specified value or business rule result, we hide or show specific ribbon buttons.

The reason I have split the execution onto two functions is because the first function called is using the CRM API, while the second function called from the previous one is done using the HTML DOM.

See also

▸ Information on HTLM DOM can be found at w3schools `http://www.w3schools.com/htmldom/default.asp`.

▸ Using JavaScript with the HTML DOM is described also at w3schools `http://www.w3schools.com/jsref/default.asp`.

▸ Additional details on ribbon customization can be found on MSDN at `http://msdn.microsoft.com/en-us/library/gg309639.aspx`.

9
Extending CRM Using Community JavaScript Libraries

In this chapter, we will cover the following:

- ▸ Using jQuery with Dynamics CRM for page element selection
- ▸ Using jQuery and CSS
- ▸ Animating form elements with jQuery
- ▸ Using jQuery UI for user interaction
- ▸ Using jQuery UI for customizations
- ▸ Integrating jQuery UI widgets
- ▸ Using `LiveValidation` for input validation as you type
- ▸ Using `Datejs` for date manipulation

Introduction

This chapter focuses on using additional JavaScript libraries or frameworks to extend your CRM environment. While they are not officially supported they do work just fine. The reason they are not supported is because the onus is on the group maintaining these libraries to produce code that does not behave unexpectedly. These libraries are doing nothing more than manipulating standard HTML on a page, and thus they can be used with any other web application.

JQuery is one of the most common, popular, and used JavaScript libraries in web development. A large number of sites are implementing it in one form or another. The support is excellent, and there is a lot of documentation and examples online and in various books. This chapter will not teach you how to use jQuery, but rather it will focus on a few examples of the most basic and common elements from the library that interacts really well and easily with your CRM environment.

The other libraries presented in this chapter, while not as well known and commonly used, give you a few additional options to enhance the user experience within your CRM application. The focus is mostly on using CRM through the browser, and not all of these examples will work when using the Outlook client. Please test all your code in both models if you intend to release CRM as such.

 Some of these examples will work only when using Dynamics CRM from the browser. The support when using the Outlook client is more restrictive. You should always test your code in both models if you intend to release it as such, and design your forms so that the lack of some of these features when using the Outlook client does not affect the business functionality of your customizations.

A lot of the examples in this chapter focus mostly on the user experience. As such, the fact that they might not run at all when using the Outlook client should not affect the business functionality of your application.

Using jQuery with Dynamics CRM for page element selection

In this recipe we will focus our attention on the most basic action that we do on a form. We will be looking at how to select a form element in Dynamics CRM using the jQuery library.

Getting ready

First off, we need to get a hold of the jQuery library and load it on our solution as a web resource. Go to `http://www.jquery.com` and grab the latest version of the library. When navigating to the that site, on the right-hand side of the home page you will see a box that gives you the options for downloading the library. Select the production version, and click on the **Download(jQuery);** button:

A lot of resources on how to use this library are available starting from that page. If you are interested in using this library in your projects I strongly suggest you start from this location to learn more about how to use jQuery.

How to do it...

For this recipe you need access to a Dynamics CRM instance. Make sure you have at least the system customizer permission in this instance.

1. Create a new blank solution

2. Add the jQuery library to your solution as a web resource. I have set up the Provider with a prefix of `crm`, and gave the library a name of `crm_jquery`. Upload the library file using the **Upload File** field on the web resource form.

3. Add a new web resource of type **JScript**. Name it **crm_jQuerySelect**.

4. Add a function named jQuerySelect. For this example we want to select the form border for all contacts and change its color to yellow. The function will look similar to the following:

```
function jQuerySelect()
{
  $(".ms-crm-Form-Page-Main-cell").css("background-
color","#FFFF00");
}
```

5. Open the **Contact** form for edit.

6. In the form's properties, add to the **Form Libraries** the **jQuery** library and the web resource containing your function.

7. On the OnLoad event of the form add the jQuerySelect function.

8. **Save** and **Publish** the form.

9. Open a contact and observe the border color changed to yellow, as shown in the following screenshot:

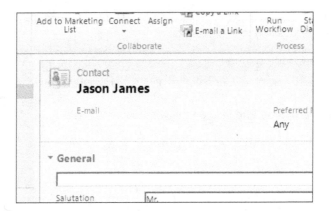

How it works...

While we have shown this functionality in a previous recipe, the purpose of this recipe is to demonstrate the fact that form elements are being selected using jQuery. The syntax used in the following line selects a specific html tag based on its class:

```
$(".ms-crm-Form-Page-Main-cell")
```

You can easily determine the ID of a form element by using the developer tools in Internet Explorer.

Be careful when performing these selections, as not all elements can be visually modified in such way. The standard Dynamics CRM CSS definitions override in some instances your selection, or overlay an image over the element background, thus blocking you from seeing your customization. Using the developer tools, you can determine where such scenarios occur on a form.

See also

▶ For additional details on jQuery syntax for form element selection see the Selectors section of the jQuery API at `http://api.jquery.com/category/selectors/`.

Using jQuery and CSS

While the previous recipe is delved into the CSS definition already, in order to actually show you some visible changes generated by your custom function, in this section we will be looking at some additional CSS changes we can implement using an external predefined CSS file that overrides the default CSS.

The most basic change, as demonstrated by the previous example, involved changing the border background color. In addition to that we can push a lot of other visual changes on to our forms. For this recipe we can take a look as using CSS to reformat the labels on the form fields that are marked as business required.

Getting ready

For this recipe we can either create a new solution, or use the one we previously created. I will be using the previous solution. The changes we will implement pertain again to the **Contact** entity, and we can reuse the same web resource to drop in an additional function.

How to do it...

So let's take a look at how we can change the label properties.

1. Open the previous solution.
2. Create a new web resource, of type **CSS**. Name it `crm_css`.
3. Add the following content to your web resource:

```
.ms-crm-Field-Required
{
  font-style: italic;
}
```

```
TD.ms-crm-Field-Required
{
  color: red;
}
```

4. Save and close your resource.

5. Open the web resource that stores our custom function.

6. Add a new function. This time our function will load our CSS web resource using jQuery:

```
function HighlightRequired()
{
    var _css = "/WebResources/crm_css";
    var cssref = document.createElement("link");
    cssref.setAttribute("rel", "stylesheet");
    cssref.setAttribute("type", "text/css");
    cssref.setAttribute("href", _css);
    $("head").append(cssref);
}
```

7. Save and close your web resource.

8. Open the contact's main form for editing.

9. Associate the `HighlightRequired` function with the `OnLoad` event of the form.

10. In addition, mark the **First Name** field as required also. By default is it business recommended.

11. Save and close the form.

12. **Publish** your solution.

13. Now open a contact and look at the two required fields on this form. The labels marked with asterisks should now be red and in italic, as shown in the following screenshot:

How it works...

There are two steps to this solution.

The first step involves creating a CSS resource that overrides the default out-of-the-box CSS definitions. In order to determine the CSS that you need to override, the Internet Explorer developer tools is your best friend. Use the selector to highlight the business required field label. On the right-hand side of the screen you will see the definition for the font.

Next, we use a JavaScript function to read the CSS resource and append it to the head area of the page. We use jQuery to do this simply because it's a single line of code.

There's more...

As mentioned in the previous recipe, using jQuery directly in a JavaScript function might not yield the expected result. That is because the default CSS could override your change. This recipe shows you how to go to the source and override the default CSS directly.

See also

▸ For additional information on formatting CSS have a look at the MSDN documentation on CSS at `http://msdn.microsoft.com/en-us/library/ie/ms531209(v=vs.85).aspx`.

Animating form elements with jQuery

Have you ever had a situation where, based on business rules, a field must become required of certain form values aligned to the rule? Let's say for example, if you select a ship to P.O. box, but there is no P.O. box information filled, then you must act and warn the user.

For the purpose of this recipe I will largely simplify this example. I will assume that we have the validation in place, and the field that needs to be filled is the **Middle Name** field. My validation will mark this field as **Business Required** on the form, but with a large number of fields, and especially when a lot of them are marked as **Business Required**, a small red star next to the name might not capture the user's attention that easily.

I could just bring up a pop-up window and let the user know that the field needs to be filled in. But that's so intrusive and so old school. With the new interactive sites nowadays, people are starting to get used to other ways of highlighting form elements.

So, my approach now is to stop the form's `OnSave` event, and to call a function that makes the required field blink once on the form.

Getting ready

For this recipe, we will continue to use the solution we have created at the beginning of the chapter. If you are starting fresh now, create a new solution. Make sure you have at least the system customizer permissions in the instance you are working in.

How to do it...

Follow these steps to make a field flash once:

1. Open the existing solution package, or create a new one. If you create a new one, add the **Contact** entity to your solution.

2. If this is a new solution package, add the **jQuery** library to your solution and to the form libraries.

3. Open the web resource that holds your JavaScript functions. If starting a new solution, create this web resource.

4. Add the following function to make a field blink:

    ```
    function BlinkMiddleName()
    {
        $("#middlename").fadeOut(3000).fadeIn(3000);}
    ```

5. Associate this function to a form event. In my case, I am associating it with the form's `OnLoad` event for the purpose of demonstration. This should, in fact, be a part of a more complex validation logic, possibly as described in the beginning of this recipe.

6. **Save** and **Publish** your solution.

7. Open a contact and observe the behavior of the field. The value is set high enough for the effect to be visible. Your animation will look as similar to the following screenshot (**Middle Name** text field fading out and back in):

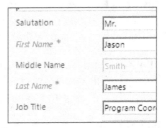

How it works...

This example uses exclusively the jQuery functionality to first select the field, and then perform the animation on it. The `fadeOut` and `fadeIn` functions take as a first parameter the time for the transition. Optionally, you can also pass as a second parameter a function delegate, thus allowing you to perform additional actions when your condition is met.

See also

► For additional animation and effect you can incorporate using jQuery see the API at `http://api.jquery.com/category/effects/`.

Using jQuery UI for user interaction

JQuery UI is an additional library based on jQuery. When using the jQuery UI, always load and reference the base jQuery library. The jQuery UI adds user interface interactions and effects to the standard jQuery library, along other features.

In order to use the jQuery UI library, proceed to the following URL and download the stable release:

```
http://jqueryui.com/
```

At the time of writing, Version v1.9.1 was the most current version, and it required jQuery version 1.6 or above. Always make sure your jQuery library is in conformance with the requirements for jQuery UI.

One of the most used widget in this library is the tooltip widget. In this recipe we will look at how to use it in the context of Dynamics CRM.

Getting ready

For this recipe we will continue to use the previously created solution package. If you are starting fresh you can create a new solution package. We will implement our customization on the **Contact** entity.

How to do it...

If we are using the previously created solution, we already have the **jQuery** library loaded as a web resource. Otherwise, you have to load it.

1. Open your existing solution.
2. Add a new web resource. Name it `crm_jqueryui`. Browse to the jQuery UI script file and load it.
3. **Save** and **Publish** your web resource.
4. Add a new web resource of type CSS. The jQuery UI comes with an associated CSS file you need to also load. Name this web resource as `crm_jqueryuicss`.
5. **Save** and **Publish** the web resource.
6. In the same web resource where we added all the previous functions, add a new function as follows:

```
function MiddleNameTooltip()
{
  var _css = "/WebResources/crm_jqueryuicss";
  var cssref = document.createElement("link");
  cssref.setAttribute("rel", "stylesheet");
```

```
    cssref.setAttribute("type", "text/css");
    cssref.setAttribute("href", _css);
    $("head").append(cssref);
    var _obj = document.getElementById("middlename_d").children[0];
    _obj.title = "";
    $("#middlename_d").tooltip({ content: "Enter your Middle Name"
});
    $("#middlename_d").tooltip({ position: {my: "left+15 center",
at: "left center"} });
    $("#middlename_d").tooltip("option", "content", "Enter your
Middle Name" );
    $("#middlename_d").tooltip("option", "position", {my: "left+15
center", at: "left center"} );
    }
```

7. Add the jQuery and jQuery UI resources to the form library.

8. Associate the `MiddleNameTooltip` function with the form's `OnLoad` event of the main contact form.

9. Save the form and close it.

10. **Save** and **Publish** your solution.

11. Now test your changes by opening a contact and pointing your mouse at the **Middle Name** field. You should see a result as shown in the following screenshot:

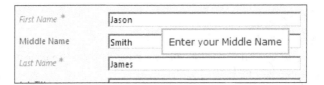

How it works...

First off, our function adds the reference to the CSS file that comes with the jQuery UI library. We load it in the head section of the form.

Next, using the standard HTML DOM we define a blank title to the field where we want to show a tooltip.

Note that defining a title with text content for a field is sufficient to make it show a tooltip using the default Dynamics CRM formatting. We are using jQuery UI in this example to take advantage of the advanced formatting of tooltip.

The following lines initialize and set the tooltip content and position. You can play around with the position to locate the tooltip at various locations relative to the page or the control with which you are associating the tooltip.

See also

▸ For information on jQuery UI see the documentation at
   `http://api.jqueryui.com/`.

▸ For additional information on the tooltip widget see the detailed description at
   `http://api.jqueryui.com/tooltip/#option-position`.

Using jQuery UI for customizations

In this recipe we will be focusing on using jQuery UI to alter the page CSS definition. I sometimes see requests for branding or customizing the color scheme of Dynamics CRM. By default this is not a supported customization. Using the jQuery library we can do some nice things with the standard look of CRM.

Getting ready

For this recipe you can either use one of the existing solutions you have previously created, or create a new one. Make sure you have at least the system customizer permission.

How to do it...

Follow these steps to add your own contact icon to the **Contact** form:

1. Open your existing solution, or create a new one.
2. Make sure the **Contact** entity is added to your solution.

3. Add a new web resource of type **png**, and upload your contact icon or an image. If you want to replace the default logo of Microsoft Dynamics CRM, make sure your image is 32 x 32 px. Name it `crm_mylogo`.

 While you can achieve this in an on-premise deployment by swapping the image file on the filesystem, this type of customization will work in both online and on-premise deployments.

4. Add a new JScript web resource. Name it `crm_logoswap`.

5. Add the following function to your web resource:

```
function LogoSwap()
{
  var _css = "/WebResources/crm_jqueryuicss";
  var cssref = document.createElement("link");
  cssref.setAttribute("rel", "stylesheet");
  cssref.setAttribute("type", "text/css");
  cssref.setAttribute("href", _css);
  $("head").append(cssref);

  var _csscustom = "/WebResources/crm_logoswapcss";
  var _cssrefcustom = document.createElement("link");
  _cssrefcustom.setAttribute("rel", "stylesheet");
  _cssrefcustom.setAttribute("type", "text/css");
  _cssrefcustom.setAttribute("href", _csscustom);
  $("head").append(_cssrefcustom);

  $("#ico_fhe_2").switchClass("ms-crm-ImageStrip-ico_fhe_2", "my-crm-ImageStrip-ico_fhe_2" );
}
```

6. Save your web resource.

7. Add a new web resource of type CSS. Name it `crm_logoswapcss`.

8. Add the following CSS definition:

```
.my-crm-ImageStrip-ico_fhe_2
{
  width: 32px;
  height: 32px;
  overflow: hidden;
  background-image: url("/WebResources/crm_mylogo");
  background-repeat: no-repeat;
  background-position-x: 0px;
  background-position-y: 0px;
  background-color: #FF0000;
}
```

9. Associate your function to the `OnLoad` event of the **Contact** form.

10. **Save** and **Publish** your solution.

11. Open a contact record and observe your change:

How it works...

In this example, we take advantage of jQuery UI to swap a CRM CSS class with our own custom class. We need to add to our solution three elements:

- ▶ Our logo image that we want to use for all contacts
- ▶ A CSS definition that will replace the default Dynamics CRM definition
- ▶ A function to load our new CSS file and using the jQuery UI `switchClass` effect to replace the image

 If you want to expand on this code, see the section where we demonstrate reading a file attached to the notes, and modify your code to automatically load a different image based on what is defined individually for each contact.

Integrating jQuery UI widgets

One of the most useful jQuery UI widgets that I have been using is the autocomplete widget. Some common scenarios for this include predefining values for both country and province in the address. Taking this approach we can minimize the risk of user input error, but also allow the user to input other values.

Getting ready

For this scenario we can use one of the previously created solutions. If one is not available, create a new solution package.

Make sure you have at least system customizer permissions to be able to perform the following operations.

How to do it...

For this example, we will predefine values for a few Canadian provinces, but we will only fill in the ones with whom we do the business. Using this approach we allow the user to add the remaining provinces for the odd times when we do something outside of the usual area.

1. Open your solution package.
2. If this is a new solution, make sure to add the jQuery, jQuery UI, and the related jQuery UI CSS files to your solution as web references.
3. Add a new web resource of type **JScript** to your solution. Name it `crm_provinceAutocomplete`.
4. Add the following function:

```
function ProvinceAutocomplete()
{
    var availableTags = [
      "Quebec",
      "Ontario",
      "Alberta",
      "British Columbia"
      ];
    $("#address1_stateorprovince").autocomplete({
      source: availableTags
    });
}
```

5. Save and close your web resource.
6. Add the **Contact** entity if not already part of your solution.

7. Open the contact's main form for editing.

8. In the form's properties, associate your custom function to the `OnLoad` event of the form.

9. Save and close the form.

10. **Save** and **Publish** your solution.

11. Test your customization by opening a contact record, and starting to type in the **Province** form field. Your results should look as shown in the following screenshot:

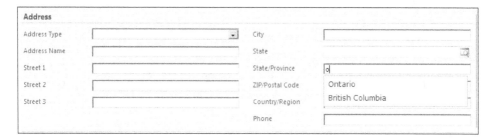

See also

▸ For additional details on the autocomplete widget see the documentation at `http://jqueryui.com/autocomplete/`.

Using LiveValidation for input validation as you type

Live Validation is a simple and efficient JavaScript library that simplifies the effort of writing your own validation routines. With simple syntax, it allows you to add multiple sets of rules to a field.

This library is open source, and is being released in two versions. For the purpose of Dynamics CRM customizations I am using the standalone version of this library.

Getting ready

For this recipe you can either create a new solution package or use one of the ones you have previously created. Make sure you have at least system customizer permissions in the environment where you will be implementing these customizations.

How to do it...

Follow these steps to add e-mail validation to an e-mail field.

 When defining a field as e-mail in Dynamics CRM, the standard e-mail validation is incomplete. While it does validate for the "@" symbol, it does not also check for an extension. For this reason it makes sense to use your own custom validation, or to use a custom library that does that.

1. Open your solution package, or create a new one if one does not exist already.
2. Add the **Contact** entity to your solution if not already added.
3. Add your jQuery web resource. We will be using this for field selection.
4. Add a new JScript web resource. Name it `crm_emailvalidation`.
5. Add the following function to your web resource:

```
function EmailLiveValidation(context)
{
  var _emailField = new LiveValidation($("#emailaddress1"));
  _emailField.add(Validate.Email);
  _emailField.add(Validate.Length, {minimum:10, maximum: 20});
}
```

6. Save and close your web resource.
7. Add a new JScript web resource. Name it `crm_livevalidation`. Add the Live Validation library.
8. Save and close this web resource.
9. Open the main contact form for editing.
10. Go to the form's properties.
11. Add in the form libraries the references to your jQuery, Live Validation, and your E-mail Validation web resource.
12. Add in the event handlers your `EmailLiveValidation` function to the `OnLoad` event of the form.
13. Save and close the form.
14. **Save** and **Publish** your solution.
15. To test your customization, open a **Contact** record, and try entering an incorrect email address in the format **me@demo**. You will observe that the standard Dynamics CRM validation allows this format to go through, but your custom validation prompts you that the format is incorrect.

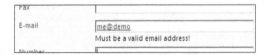

How it works...

Our script example creates a new `LiveValidation` object in the first line of code. It passes the field name as a parameter on creation.

The following lines allow us to add multiple independent rules, thus creating more complex validation scenarios. You can add as many rules as required. For example, our second rule adds a validation to check the length of the e-mail. Thus, the e-mail entered must be between 10 and 20 characters.

There's more...

This library supports all types of validations. Check the documentation available. For most of these validation rules CRM does have a counterpart. Setting up the field with a defined data type, for example, makes a lot of this library's functions unnecessary.

Some of the instances where this library becomes useful include rules around a minimum and maximum value expected in a field and matching of values.

See also

- ▸ To download the LiveValidation library use the following link:

  `http://livevalidation.com/download`

- ▸ For additional documentation on use and features of this library see the documentation at `http://livevalidation.com/documentation`.

Using Datejs for date manipulation

Datejs is another example of an open source library. It is a simple and fast library for manipulating dates.

This library is released under the MIT License. For additional details about this license limitations see the Open Source Initiative at `http://opensource.org/licenses/mit-license.php`.

The source code for this library is hosted at Google Code, and it can be found at the following URL:

`http://code.google.com/p/datejs/downloads/list`

Getting ready

First off, in order to work with this library, we need to download a copy to include in our solution package. Currently there are two versions of the library. The simple `date.js` is the en-US locale. The additional Alpha1 version includes additional locales and a few other goodies.

How to do it...

Imagine an SLA around opened cases, where all new cases have to have a response by the end of Friday of the week they were opened in. Using this library we can achieve this in almost no time at all. So let's get started.

1. Create a new solution package, or use an existing one if one is available.

2. Add a new web resource of type **JScript**. Name it `crm_datejs`. Browse to the `date.js` library and load it.

3. Save and close your web resource.

4. Add a new web resource of type **JScript**. Name it `crm_mydateprocess`.

5. Add the following function to this web resource:

```
function FindFriday()
{
   var _actDate = Xrm.Page.getAttribute("crm_actdate").getValue();
   if(_actDate == null || _actDate == "")
   {
      Xrm.Page.getAttribute("crm_actdate").setValue(Date.today().
next().friday());
   }
}
```

6. Save and close your web resource.

7. Add the **Case** entity to your solution.

8. Open the Case main form for editing.

9. Add a new field of type **Date** and **Time** to your form. Format it as **Date Only**, and name it `crm_actdate`.

10. Save your form.

11. In form's properties, in the Form Libraries add your `crm_datejs` reference and a reference to the `crm_mydateprocess` web resources.

12. In the event handlers associate to the `OnLoad` form event your `FindFriday` function.

13. Save and close your **Case** form.

14. Publish all your solution package customizations.

15. Now test your customizations by opening a case form. You will see the **Act Date** field populated with the date of the next Friday.

How it works...

Our function simply checks when a case form is opened if the **Act Date** is filled in, and if not it populates the date of next coming Friday.

The `date.js` library simplifies all the logic of finding specific days and working with dates. For additional details on the features of this library look at the documentation and examples provided on their website.

There's more...

Using the `date.js` library will greatly reduce the time you spend working with dates. From finding a specific day in the week, to navigating a specific number of days back and forth in time, all you need in most cases is a single line of code. The syntax is simple and easy to remember, and in the context of Dynamics CRM the library behaves well.

See also

▶ To download the `date.js` library go to `http://code.google.com/p/datejs/downloads/list`.

▶ For additional instructions on how to use this library see the getting started guide at `http://www.datejs.com/2007/11/27/getting-started-with-datejs/`.

▶ For additional details on the MIT license model see OSI site at `http://opensource.org/licenses/mit-license.php`.

10
Light Social Media Integration

In this chapter, we will cover the following topics:

- ▶ Integrating with Facebook
- ▶ Integrating accounts with LinkedIn
- ▶ Integrating contacts with LinkedIn
- ▶ Adding Twitter feeds
- ▶ Working with Del.icio.us data

Introduction

While the focus of the previous chapters has been mostly on customizing Dynamics CRM and using data internal to the application, this chapter will focus on bringing various other data feeds into the application.

This chapter is a light approach to integrating various social media sources into Dynamics CRM 2011. We will only focus on the client-side scripting aspect. You can do a lot more by using plugins, but the value brought by integrating other sources on the client side is, in many instances, more than enough. It also shifts the load from the server to the client, which in some instances is a desirable outcome.

In order for all of these recipes to work, the machine you are developing on, as well as the client machines need to have direct access to the internet. No caching takes place, and all data is retrieved dynamically from external sources.

 When taking this approach to customization, make sure that the client machines have access to the internet, as well as to the development/test machine.

Integrating with Facebook

In this recipe, we will be looking at the most simplistic way to bring Facebook information into your CRM. We are doing this exclusively on the client side, thus adding no additional load on server resource. For this reason, the client machine will need to have internet access, and the access to Facebook should not be blocked by the corporate firewall.

We will be taking advantage of the **Facebook Badge** feature. If you go to `http://www.facebook.com/badges/`, you will find the available badge options. For this example, I will focus on using the **Profile badge**. We will capture the contact information as it relates to Facebook from the system user, and we will display a Profile badge on the **Contact** form.

Getting ready

You will need access to a Dynamics CRM 2011 instance. In addition, you will need the system customizer or system administrator permissions.

If you do not have a solution package already created, you should create one for this chapter.

You can use either a CRM Online instance or an On-Premise deployment for this solution. If you are using On-Premise, make sure that the user machines have direct access to the internet, and that the Facebook site is not being blocked or filtered by the corporate firewall.

Also, if you are accessing the corporate CRM instance through a VPN connection and if the connection drops your internet connection while the VPN is active, then this recipe will not work. Please work with the network infrastructure team supporting your final production deployment to make sure this is a supported scenario.

How to do it...

In order to add a Profile badge on the **Contact** entity, perform the following steps:

1. Open any existing solution you might have, or create a new one.
2. Add the **Contact** entity to your solution.

3. Add a new web resource of type **JScript**. Name it `FacebookScript` (new_facebookscript).

4. Add the following function to this resource:

```
function getFacebookBadge()
{
   var _fbURL = Xrm.Page.getAttribute("new_facebookurl").
getValue();

   if(_fbURL != null && _fbURL != "")
   {
      var _fbuser = _fbURL.substring(_fbURL.indexOf("facebook.com/")
+ 13);

      $("#new_facebookurl_d").append("<a href='"+_fbURL+"'
target='_blank'><img src='http://graph.facebook.com/"+_fbuser+"/
picture?type=normal'/></a>");
   }
}
```

5. **Save and Close** this web resource.

6. Add a new web resource of type **JScript**. Name it `jQuery` and load the latest jQuery library available at `http://jquery.com/`.

7. **Save and Close** this web resource.

8. Open the **Contact** main form for editing.

9. In **Form Properties** add the `jQuery` resource to the **Form Libraries**.

10. Click on **OK** to close **Form Properties**.

11. Add a new section to your form. Label it `Facebook Badge` and check the **Show the label of this section on the Form** and **Show a line at top of the section** checkboxes.

12. On the **Formatting** tab, set the properties to **Two Columns**. You will want to adjust this based on the size of the badge created.

 You can pull the profile image in various sizes from Facebook. The options to pass are square, small, normal, and large.

13. Click on **OK** to close the **Section Properties**.

14. In this section add a new **Single Line of Text** field. Set its format to **URL** and name it `Facebook URL` (new_facebookurl).

15. Add the field to the form and in the **Formatting** tab set the layout to **Two Columns**.

16. Click on **OK** to close the **Field Properties** window.

17. Add your function to the `OnChange` event of the **new_facebookurl** field.

18. Also add your function to the form's `OnLoad` event.

19. **Save and Close** the form.

20. Publish your solution.

21. In order to test this customization, open an existing contact or add a new one.

22. Retrieve the URL of the contact's profile from Facebook. This URL is in the `http://www.facebook.com/username` format.

23. Put this URL in the **new_facebookurl** field. Once you tab out of the field, the script will execute and will bring the contact's image over.

24. This method works with both **Contacts** and **Accounts**. The standard URL used for both is of the same format.

How it works...

This integration method brings over the profile picture of the contact or account, as presented and maintained on Facebook by the owner. While for companies (accounts), it's almost guaranteed to get a logo or a relevant image, when using this approach with contacts be aware that since Facebook is not really a professional network, some images retrieved might not present the person in a professional way.

There's more...

In addition to retrieving the logo image of a contact or account, using the Graph API you can retrieve additional information. For details on using the Graph API, see the Facebook Developers documentation at `http://developers.facebook.com/docs/reference/api/`.

See also

▶ jQuery library and documentation at `http://jquery.com/`.

Integrating accounts with LinkedIn

Pulling a company profile from the data they maintain is always a better idea than having to maintain that information yourself. While we won't be able to have all customers update all the profile information we need to track, bringing in some information from their public profiles will always make things easier on our team.

In this recipe we will look at a simple way of bringing a customer's LinkedIn card information on their profile page. In addition, this pull of data happens exclusively on the client side.

[Always check with the data provider to determine if the terms of use allow you to implement this kind of customization in your specific scenario.]

Getting ready

In order to test this solution, you will need access to a Dynamics CRM instance and be a part of system customizer or system administrator permission.

You can create a new solution package or reuse an existing one.

How to do it...

Perform the following steps to add the LinkedIn company card to your CRM **Account** form:

1. Create a new solution package if one is not already available.
2. Add the **Account** entity to your solution.
3. Open the **Account** main form to edit.
4. Make the **Account Name** field span two columns. This way the full card width can be displayed right underneath the account name.
5. **Save and Close** the form.
6. Add a new web resource of type **JScript**. Name it `LinkedIn Company Profile` (`new_LinkedInCompanyProfile`).
7. Add the following function to your web resource:

```
function LinkedInCompanyProfile()
{
    var _companyName = Xrm.Page.getAttribute("name").getValue();

    if(_companyName != null && _companyName != "")
    {
        while(_companyName.indexOf(" ") != -1)
```

```
        {
          _companyName = _companyName.replace(" ", "-");
        }
        _companyName = _companyName.toLowerCase();
        $("#name").after(function(){
          var script = '<script src="http://platform.linkedin.com/
in.js" type="text/javascript"></script>' +
          '<script type="IN/CompanyProfile" data-id="' + _companyName
+
          '" data-format="inline" data-related="false"></script>';
          return script;
        });
      }
    }
```

8. **Save and Close** your web resource.

9. Add a new web resource of type **JScript**. Name it jQuery (new_jquery).

10. Load the jQuery library in this web resource.

11. **Save and Close** the web resource.

12. Return to the **Account** main form.

13. Add to the **Form Properties** a reference to the jQuery resource.

14. Also add a reference to the LinkedIn Company Profile web resource.

15. In the form's OnLoad event handler, add a reference to your LinkedInCompanyProfile() function.

16. Click on **OK** to close the **Form Properties**.

17. On the account name's **Field Properties**, add a new event handler for the OnChange event, and reference your LinkedInCompanyProfile() function.

18. Click on **OK** to close the **Field Properties** window.

19. **Save and Close** the **Account** form.

20. **Save** and **Publish** your solution.

21. Open an account record. If no account record is in there in the system, create a new one.

22. Once a record is retrieved, the company LinkedIn profile card is displayed if the company profile is found on LinkedIn.

How it works...

Using the value of **Account Name** defined as the name of the company, this script retrieves the company card from LinkedIn and displays it on the form, right under the **Account Name** field. With it, you get a link back to the company profile in LinkedIn, along with the company name, the logo, and a short description.

> Please be aware that this functionality does not perform a search of companies on LinkedIn, but rather it looks-up a company by its exact name defined in the **Account Name** field. For situations where the stored account name is different than the company name defined in the LinkedIn profile, a new custom field can be created to capture the publicly available company name.

There's more...

This example uses jQuery only for page location and to insert the actual card after the account name. You could easily change the location of the company card by selecting any other tag on the page.

See also

▶ For additional information on the jQuery functions used in this script see the following links:

  ❑ http://api.jquery.com/category/selectors/

  ❑ http://api.jquery.com/append/

▶ For information on the LinkedIn JavaScript API see the developer resources at https://developer.linkedin.com/javascript.

Integrating contacts with LinkedIn

Similar to the approach we took in pulling account information from LinkedIn, we can handle the contacts. The difference is, due to the higher probability of having identical names, we can handle this by asking the system user for some additional information.

You could build a more complex solution that queries based on the first, middle, and last names, and returns all matches for the user to select the correct contact; but that would be a next-level solution, and I would probably consider doing it in something other than JavaScript.

In this solution, I will only ask the system user to input the URL to LinkedIn user profile. From there, I will retrieve the required information and bring in a user profile card.

 Always check with the data provider to determine if the terms of use allow you to implement this kind of customization in your specific scenario.

Getting ready

In order to build this recipe you will need access to a Dynamics CRM instance, as well as have a system customizer or system administrator permission.

In addition, you should create a solution package if one is not already available.

How to do it...

Within your solution package, take the following steps to customize this:

1. Add the **Contact** entity to your solution, if not already added.

2. Create a new web resource of type **JScript**. Name it `LinkedIn Contact Profile` (`new_linkedincontactprofile`).

3. Add the following function to your script file:

```
function LinkedInGetContactProfile()
{
  var _contactProfile = Xrm.Page.getAttribute("new_linkedinurl").
getValue();

  if(_contactProfile != null && _contactProfile != "")
  {
    _contactProfile = _contactProfile.substring(_contactProfile.
indexOf("linkedin.com/in/")+16, _contactProfile.length+1);

    $("#new_linkedinurl").after(function(){
```

```
        var script = '<script src="http://platform.linkedin.com/
    in.js" type="text/javascript"></script>' +
        '<script type="IN/MemberProfile" data-id="www.linkedin.com/
    in/' + _contactProfile +
        '" data-format="inline" data-related="false"></script>';
        return script;
    });
    }
}
```

4. **Save and Close** the web resource.

5. Create a new web resource of type **JScript**. Name it jQuery (new_jquery).

6. Load the most recent jQuery library you have available.

7. **Save and Close** the web resource.

8. Open the **Contact** main form for editing.

9. Add a new one-column section. Label it LinkedIn Profile.

10. Check the **Show the label of this section on the Form** and the **Show a line at top of the section** checkboxes as shown in the following screenshot:.

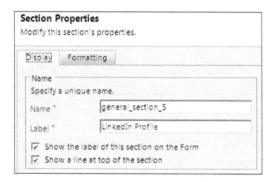

11. Leave the **Formatting** to **One Column**.

12. Click on **OK** to close this window.

13. Add a new **Text** field. Name it LinkedIn URL (new_linkedinurl). Set the **Format** to **URL**.

14. Add the field to the section we created previously.

15. On the **Form Properties**, in **Form Libraries**, add first a reference to the jQuery library.

16. Then add a reference to the LinkedIn Contact Profile library that contains our function.

17. In the **Event Handlers** section, add a reference to your LinkedInGetContactProfile() function to the form OnLoad event.

18. Click on **OK** to close the **Form Properties** window.

19. In the **LinkedIn URL** field properties, on the **Events** tab, add a reference to the same function to the `OnChange` field event.

20. Click on **OK** to close the **Field Properties** window.

21. **Save and Close** the **Account** form.

22. In your solution package, click on **Publish All Customizations**.

23. In order to test this, first off, let's open a new browser window and run a search for *linkedin firstname lastname* where *firstname* and *lastname* are the names of a contact you are looking for. This will return their public LinkedIn profile page.

24. The URL format of this page is in the following format:

    `http://www.linkedin.com/in/nicolaetarla`

25. Copy this URL into the **Contact** page in the **LinkedIn URL** field we created.

26. Once you tab out of this field, the script will run and the following information card will be displayed on the **Contact** form:

How it works...

As mentioned at the beginning of this recipe, in this instance we will have the system user do a little bit of leg work. They have to retrieve the contact's public profile. That is an easy enough task using any search engine available and also greatly simplifies the process of sifting through possible multiple users with the same name.

The first part of the script strips out the member name, which could potentially be used in other scenarios. The second part is the standard code presented in the member profile plugin generator.

See also

▶ For additional details on the plugins provided by LinkedIn see the documentation at `https://developer.linkedin.com/plugins`.

▶ For the member profile plugin generator, see the link `https://developer.linkedin.com/plugins/member-profile-plugin-generator`.

Adding Twitter feeds

Associating your customers' or contacts' Twitter information to your CRM can sometimes bring valuable information to the fingertips of your sales staff. While there are more advanced solutions that can process the tweet feeds on the server and provide caching, the very light solution I am going to demonstrate is client-side only, and does not add any additional load to the server. Furthermore, it could be the preferred approach for IFD deployments, where the majority of users access CRM remotely, whether from home, office, or on the road. This way, you are pushing all that transfer off your network.

We will be using the **twitterjs** library to assist in the call to retrieve the recent tweets.

Getting ready

For this recipe, you must have access to a Dynamics CRM instance, and have either a system customizer or system administrator permission.

If you do not have a solution package already created, create a new one as described in the initial chapters of this book.

We will capture the Twitter handle of a customer on the **Account** form, and using that, we will retrieve the last ten tweets of that customer.

How to do it...

In order to implement this customization, we should be working within a solution package. You can either create a new one or use an existing one.

1. Add the **Account** entity to your solution if not already added.

2. Open the **Account** main form for editing.

3. Add a new section to your form. I formatted it as **One Column** and labeled it `Twitter`. Select the **Show the label of this section on the Form** and the **Show a line at top of the section** checkboxes.

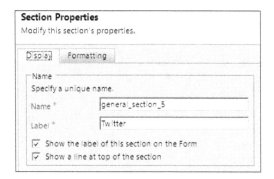

4. Add a new **Text** field named `Twitter Handle` (`new_twitter`).

5. Add your field to the form, in the previously section created.

6. **Save and Close** the form.

7. Create a web resource of type **JScript**. Name it `jQuery` (`new_jquery`).

8. Load the jQuery library.

9. **Save and Close** the form.

10. Create a new web resource of type **JScript**. Name it `TwitterJS` (`new_twitterjs`) and load the twitterjs library.

11. **Save and Close** the form.

12. Create another web resource of type **JScript**. Name it `Twitter` (`new_twitter`).

13. Load the following function:

```
function getTweets()
{
   var _twitterHandle = Xrm.Page.getAttribute("new_twitter").
getValue();

   if(_twitterHandle != null && _twitterHandle != "")
   {
     JQTWEET = {
     user: _twitterHandle,
     numTweets: 10,

     loadTweets: function() {
       $.ajax({
         url: 'http://api.twitter.com/1/statuses/user_timeline.
json/',
         type: 'GET',
         dataType: 'jsonp',
         data: {
           screen_name: JQTWEET.user,
           include_rts: true,
           count: JQTWEET.numTweets,
           include_entities: true
           },
         success: function(data, textStatus, xhr) {
           var _myhtml = "";
           for (var i = 0; i < data.length; i++) {
               _myhtml += "<div class='tweet'>" + data[i].text + "</
div><br />";
           }
           $('#new_twitter_d').append(_myhtml);
```

```
        }
      });
    }
  };

  JQTWEET.loadTweets();

}
else
{
  return;
}
}
```

14. **Save and Close** the page.

15. Go back to editing the **Account** main form.

16. In the **Form Properties** window, on the **Events** tab, in the **Form Libraries** section, add the **jQuery**, **TwitterJS**, and the **Twitter** web resources in this order.

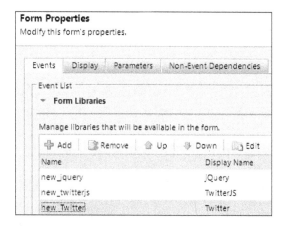

17. In the **Event Handlers** section, on the **Form OnLoad**, add your **getTweets** function.

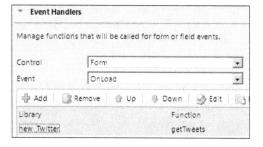

18. Click on **OK** to close the **Form Properties** window.

19. On the **Twitter Handle** text field you have created and added to the form, add the same **getTweets** function to the **OnChange** event handler.

20. Click on **OK** to close the **Field Properties** window.

21. **Save and Close** the **Account** form.

22. **Save** and **Publish** your solution package.

23. To test the customization, open an account. If no Twitter handle is present, add one in the **Twitter Handle** field. Once you leave this field, the last ten messages in the feed are retrieved and displayed on the form, as seen in the following screenshot:

24. Next time when you open this account, the query will run again and retrieve ten new messages if any new ones have been posted since you last opened it.

How it works...

Using the `tweet.js` library simplifies our call to retrieve the tweeter feed. The syntax is customizable, and you can even configure a generic system-wide setting to define the number of most recent tweets to be retrieved by populating the `numTweets: 10` with a different value store in a settings area.

On a successful call, we are looping through the ten tweets retrieved and generating our HTML to arrange the tweets in the page.

Of course, this is only a pretty simplistic example on how to retrieve the tweet feed and how to display it on the form. From here on we can do additional work with the HTML formatting and make the result look much better.

Adding CSS

One thing we can do to make it more visually appealing is we can define a CSS resource to format our feed. We can color the background of each feed or highlight certain terms. For examples on referencing a CSS resource, see the *Using jQuery and CSS* recipe in *Chapter 9, Extending CRM using Community JavaScript Libraries*.

Parsing URLs

Another example of increased usability is to parse the formatted HTML and to turn URLs into proper hyperlinks. We will not delve any deeper into this example as this is standard JavaScript and HTML functionality, independent of Dynamics CRM.

Parsing Tweeter handles

Yet another way to increase usability is to parse the actual handles that appear in tweets, and to pre-define an action. For example, you can turn each handle into a hyperlink pointing you to that handle owner's feed. Again, the code for this is independent of Dynamics CRM, and it's only JavaScript and HTML.

▸   For additional details and to get the twitterjs library, go to Google Project at `http://code.google.com/p/twitterjs/`.

Working with Del.icio.us data

In this recipe, we will have a quick look at leveraging a tagging site such as Del.icio.us to determine the popularity of an account. If you intend to use this in a production environment I would suggest relying on a combination of multiple sources. Take this result with a grain of salt, unless your business revolves around this. This example is only to show you how you can get data from Del.icio.us and use it within Dynamics CRM. You can expand on this example and retrieve the actual tags of a specific account or any other information stored on Del.icio.us.

 The updated URL now for Del.icio.us is `www.delicious.com`, but for most of us who have used it since the inception, `del.icio.us` still rings the bell.

Getting ready

For this recipe you will need the jQuery library. Head over to `http://jquery.com/` and grab the latest version from there.

Make sure you have the system customizer or system administrator permission in the environment you will be developing in.

You can re-use a previously created solution package, or create a new one.

How to do it...

As previously described in other recipes, you will need the jQuery library. Assuming you have downloaded it already, perform the following steps:

1. Open your solution package, or create a new one if one doesn't already exist.
2. Add a new web resource of type **JScript**. Name it `jQuery` and load the jQuery library.
3. **Save** and **Publish** your resource.
4. Add the **Account** entity to your solution package if not already added.
5. Open the **Account** main form for editing.
6. Add a new text field to store the popularity index value returned by our function. Make this a read-only field and name it `Del.icio.us index (new_popularity)`.

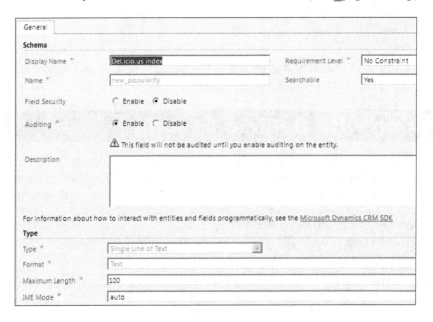

7. Save and add this field to the form.

8. Add to the form properties on the **OnLoad**, a reference to your **getDelicious** function.

9. Also, on the **OnChange** event of the **Web Site (websiteurl)** field, add a reference to the same **getDelicious** function.

10. **Save** and **Publish** your form.

11. Add a new web resource of type **JScript**. Name it `new_delicious`.

12. Add the following function to your web resource:

```
function getDelicious()
{
   var _deliciousURL = Xrm.Page.getAttribute("websiteurl").
getValue();
   if(_deliciousURL != null && _deliciousURL != "")
   {
     $.ajax({
       type: "GET",
       dataType: "json",
       url: "http://feeds.delicious.com/v2/json/urlinfo/
data?url="+_deliciousURL+"&amp;callback=?",
       success: function(data){
         var count = 0;
         if (data.length > 0) {
           count = data[0].total_posts;
         }
Xrm.Page.getAttribute("new_popularity").setValue(count.tString());
       }
     });
   }
}
```

13. **Save** and **Publish** your web resource.

14. In order to test, open an account and make sure that it has a website populated. If not, add a website.

15. Your **De.icio.us index field** will populate with the bookmark count of that URL from Del.icio.us.

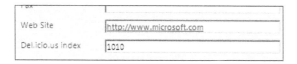

How it works...

We are calling our function in two places in this example, to make sure we bring an updated bookmark count every time the URL changes or when a user opens an existing account.

Our function queries the Del.icio.us API and retrieves the total number of bookmarks for the specified URL. We are using jQuery Ajax for the call.

There's more...

Using a similar approach, you can query for additional information from Del.icio.us. You might want to query specific tags or even all the posts of an account or contact if they have an account on that system.

See also

▸ For additional details on working with Del.icio.us see the developer documentation at `http://delicious.com/developers`.

Index

Process in Dynamics CRM 2011 30
Profile badge
  about 230
  adding, to Contact entity 230-232
provider
  request, re-routing to 74

Q

Qualify Lead button
  hiding, on Lead entity 186, 187

R

RangeError 112
  generating 116
rating gauge field
  creating 162-164
record
  progression process, enhancing 200
ReferenceError 112
  generating 116
request
  re-routing, to provider 74
resources
  creating 29
  managing 29
review
  accounts, making for 172, 174
ribbon
  about 182
  elements 182
  used, for displaying information 200-206
ribbon artefacts
  creating 194-197
  removing 185-187
ribbon button
  adding, at web application level 182-184
  adding, to entity 185
  removing, dynamically 198-200
  workflow, starting from 188, 189
RibbonCustomization 182

S

SaaS model 9
Save and Close functionality 120

Save and New button 120
Save functionality 120
scripting 7
scripts
  about 26
  creating 27, 28
  managing 27, 28
sections
  flagging, for user 165, 166
  working with 96-98
security roles
  about 40
  adding, steps 40, 41
ShowContactPicture() function 170
solution model
  managed solution 12
  unmanaged solution 12
solution package 10
solutions
  creating 10, 11
  removing 11
  URL 12
  used, for packaging 10, 11
State example
  expanding 62
State/Province relationship
  versus Country/Region relationship 49
SyntaxError 112
  generating 117
system customizer role 10

T

tabs
  working with 96-98
TabStateChange event 86
text fields
  about 43
  information, writing back to 50
  working with 44-49
ticker symbol field
  about 72
  validating 72-74
tracing
  IE, using for 140-142
try catch finally block 136

Thank you for buying
Microsoft Dynamics CRM 2011 Scripting Cookbook

About Packt Publishing

Packt, pronounced 'packed', published its first book "*Mastering phpMyAdmin for Effective MySQL Management*" in April 2004 and subsequently continued to specialize in publishing highly focused books on specific technologies and solutions.

Our books and publications share the experiences of your fellow IT professionals in adapting and customizing today's systems, applications, and frameworks. Our solution-based books give you the knowledge and power to customize the software and technologies you're using to get the job done. Packt books are more specific and less general than the IT books you have seen in the past. Our unique business model allows us to bring you more focused information, giving you more of what you need to know, and less of what you don't.

Packt is a modern, yet unique publishing company, which focuses on producing quality, cutting-edge books for communities of developers, administrators, and newbies alike. For more information, please visit our website: www.PacktPub.com.

About Packt Enterprise

In 2010, Packt launched two new brands, Packt Enterprise and Packt Open Source, in order to continue its focus on specialization. This book is part of the Packt Enterprise brand, home to books published on enterprise software – software created by major vendors, including (but not limited to) IBM, Microsoft and Oracle, often for use in other corporations. Its titles will offer information relevant to a range of users of this software, including administrators, developers, architects, and end users.

Writing for Packt

We welcome all inquiries from people who are interested in authoring. Book proposals should be sent to author@packtpub.com. If your book idea is still at an early stage and you would like to discuss it first before writing a formal book proposal, contact us; one of our commissioning editors will get in touch with you.

We're not just looking for published authors; if you have strong technical skills but no writing experience, our experienced editors can help you develop a writing career, or simply get some additional reward for your expertise.

Microsoft Dynamics AX 2012 Development Cookbook

Solve real-world Microsoft Dynamics AX development problems with over 80 practical recipes

Mindaugas Pocius

Microsoft Dynamics AX 2012 Development Cookbook

ISBN: 978-1-849684-64-4   Paperback: 372 pages

Solve real-world Microsoft Dynamics AX development problems with over 80 practical recipes

1. Develop powerful, successful Dynamics AX projects with efficient X++ code with this book and eBook

2. Proven recipes that can be reused in numerous successful Dynamics AX projects

3. Covers general ledger, accounts payable, accounts receivable, project modules and general functionality of Dynamics AX

(MCTS): Microsoft BizTalk Server 2010 (70-595) Certification Guide

Johan Hedberg   Kent Weare
Morten la Cour

(MCTS): Microsoft BizTalk Server 2010 (70-595) Certification Guide

ISBN: 978-1-849684-92-7   Paperback: 476 pages

A compact certification guide to help you prepare for the pass exam 70-595: TS Developing Business Process and Integration Solutions by using Microsoft Biz Talk Server 2010

1. This book and e-book will provide all that you need to know in order to pass the (70-595) Developing Business Process and Integration Solutions exam by Using Microsoft BizTalk Server 2010 book

2. The layout and content of the book closely matches that of the skills measured by the exam, which makes it easy to focus your learning and maximize your study time in areas where you need improvement.

Please check **www.PacktPub.com** for information on our titles

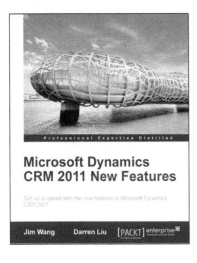

Microsoft Dynamics CRM 2011 New Features

ISBN: 978-1-849682-06-0   Paperback: 288 pages

Get up to speed with the new features of Microsoft Dynamics CRM 2011

1. Master the new features of Microsoft Dynamics 2011

2. Use client-side programming to perform data validation, automation, and process enhancement

3. Learn powerful event driven server-side programming methods: Plug-Ins and Processes (Formerly Workflows)

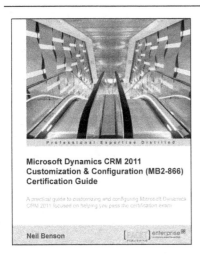

Microsoft Dynamics CRM 2011 Customization & Configuration (MB2-866) Certification Guide

ISBN: 978-1-849685-80-1   Paperback: 306 pages

A partical guide to customizing and configuring Microsoft Dynamics CRM 2011 focused on helping you pass the certification exam

1. Based on the official syllabus for course 80294B to help prepare you for the MB2-866 exam

2. Filled with all the procedures you need to know to pass the exam including screenshots

3. Take the practice exam with 75 sample questions to assess your knowledge before you sit the real exam

Please check **www.PacktPub.com** for information on our titles

www.ingramcontent.com/pod-product-compliance
Lightning Source LLC
LaVergne TN
LVHW062310060326
832902LV00013B/2148